THE MAIN EVENT

MEMBER RECIPES

Cooking Club
of
America

Minnetonka, Minnesota

THE MAIN EVENT/MEMBER RECIPES

Tom Carpenter
Creative Director

Jennifer Guinea
Senior Book Development Coordinator

Jenya Prosmitsky
Book Design and Production

Lisa Golden Schroeder
Recipe Editor

Phil Aarrestad
Commissioned Photography

Robin Krause
Food Stylist

Susan Telleen
Assistant Food Stylist

On Cover: Roast Quail with Dried Fruit Stuffing, page 15.

On Page 1: Tenderloin of Beef, page 26.

4 5 6 7 8 /06 05 04 03

ISBN 1-58159-139-X

Cooking Club of America
12301 Whitewater Drive
Minnetonka, MN 55343
www.cookingclub.com

The Cooking Club of America proudly presents this special cookbook edition which includes the personal favorites of your fellow Members. Each recipe has been screened by a cooking professional and edited for clarity; most were kitchen tested. However, we are not able to kitchen-test every recipe and cannot guarantee their outcome, or your safety in their preparation or consumption. Please be advised that any recipes which require the use of dangerous equipment (such as pressure cookers) or potentially unsafe preparation procedures (such as canning and pickling), should be used with caution and safe, healthy practices.

CONTENTS

INTRODUCTION

And now, for our
MAIN EVENT

The question has to be as old as cooking itself: "What's for dinner?" Of course, every meal isn't dinner, so the gist might be: "What are we eating?"

However the question is posed, or whatever the meal occasion, the answer never hesitates. It always centers on the main dish, the feature component of the meal, the focus food around which everything else—appetizers, salads, side dishes, breads, desserts—hovers.

And everyone can use more ideas to add to their cooking repertoire: feature recipes that will expand your culinary horizons while adding wonderful taste and exciting variety to your table.

That's why we asked Cooking Club of America Members to share their main dish (Main Event) ideas with other club members. The results take life on the pages that follow—254 recipes spread over topics such as Company's Coming, Sizzling Grilling, Poultry Plus, Perfect Pasta, Comforting One-Dish Dinners and much more.

When it's time to create an interesting new dish—or look for some intriguing twists on great old ideas—look no further than this book of Main Event member recipes.

Cooking Club
of
America®

COMPANY'S COMING

CHRISTMAS MORNING STRATA

David A. Heppner
Brandon, Florida

1 tablespoon oil
1 lb. ground pork sausage
2 teaspoons mustard
6 slices white sandwich bread, crusts removed, cut into 1-inch cubes
2 cups (8 oz.) shredded Swiss cheese
$1^1/_2$ cups milk
3 large eggs, lightly beaten
$^1/_2$ teaspoon Worcestershire sauce
$^1/_8$ teaspoon salt
$^1/_8$ teaspoon freshly ground pepper
$^1/_8$ teaspoon nutmeg

1. Heat oven to 350°F. Spray 3-quart casserole with nonstick cooking spray.

2. In large skillet, heat oil over medium-high heat until hot. Cook until sausage is brown and crumbles; drain well. Stir in mustard; mix well. Pour mixture into casserole. Top with bread crumbs and cheese.

3. In large bowl, combine milk, eggs, Worcestershire sauce, salt, pepper and nutmeg; mix well. Pour mixture over bread and cheese. Cover and refrigerate 8 hours.

4. Bake, uncovered, 50 minutes or until set.

6 servings.

CRAB SOUFFLE

Kathy Hickey
Ashley, Pennsylvania

1 (6-oz.) pkg. crabmeat, juice reserved
1 cup (4 oz.) shredded cheddar cheese
2 tablespoons butter
1 cup chopped green onions
5 tablespoons all-purpose flour
1 teaspoon salt
$^1/_2$ teaspoon freshly ground pepper
1 cup half-and-half
Dash cayenne pepper
6 eggs, separated
Dash cream of tartar

1. Heat oven to 375°F. Spray 3-quart casserole with nonstick cooking spray.

2. In large bowl, combine crabmeat and cheese; blend well. Set aside.

3. In large skillet, melt butter over medium heat. Sauté onions until soft. Stir in flour, salt, pepper and half-and-half; simmer until thick. Add cayenne pepper and reserved crab juice. Stir in egg yolks.

4. In large bowl, combine egg whites with crabmeat mixture. Beat mixture at medium speed until smooth. Add cream of tartar; continue beating at medium speed until stiff peaks form.

5. Fold one portion of egg white mixture into butter mixture; stir gently. Slowly fold in remaining egg white mixture.

6. Pour mixture into casserole. Bake 45 minutes or until set. Serve with hot rolls, if desired.

6 servings.

LAYERED PICNIC SANDWICHES

Tammy Raynes
Natchitoches, Louisiana

2 (1-lb.) loaves Italian bread
$^1/_4$ cup olive oil
3 garlic cloves, minced
2 teaspoons Italian seasoning
$^1/_2$ lb. sliced deli roast beef
$^3/_4$ lb. sliced mozzarella cheese
2 tablespoons chopped fresh basil
3 medium tomatoes, thinly sliced
$^1/_4$ lb. thinly sliced salami
1 (6.5-oz.) jar marinated artichoke
   hearts, drained, sliced
1 (10-oz.) pkg. mixed salad greens
$^1/_2$ lb. sliced deli chicken
1 medium onion, thinly sliced
$^1/_4$ teaspoon salt
$^1/_8$ teaspoon freshly ground pepper

1. Cut loaves in half horizontally; hollow out tops and bottoms, leaving $^1/_2$-inch shells. Reserve soft bread for another use.

2. In small bowl, combine oil and garlic; mix well. Brush mixture inside of bread shells. Sprinkle with 1 teaspoon of the Italian seasoning.

3. Layer bottom of each loaf with $^1/_4$ of the roast beef, mozzarella, basil, tomatoes, salami, artichokes, salad greens, chicken and onion. Repeat layers. Season with salt, pepper and remaining 1 teaspoon Italian seasoning.

4. Replace bread tops; wrap tightly in plastic wrap. Refrigerate at least 1 hour before serving. Slice to serve.

12 servings.

CRAB QUICHE

Tammy Raynes
Natchitoches, Louisiana

2 eggs
$^1/_2$ cup mayonnaise
2 tablespoons all-purpose flour
$^1/_2$ cup milk
2 (6-oz.) cans crabmeat, drained
$^1/_3$ cup chopped green onions
1 tablespoon minced fresh parsley
2 cups (8 oz.) shredded Swiss cheese
1 (9-inch) unbaked pie shell

1. Heat oven to 350°F. Spray 9-inch pie plate with nonstick cooking spray.

2. In medium bowl, beat eggs at medium speed until frothy. Stir in mayonnaise, flour and milk; mix well Stir in crabmeat, green onions, parsley and cheese; mix well.

3. Place pie shell in plate. Spoon mixture into pie shell. Bake 1 hour or until set.

6 to 8 servings.

LOW COUNTRY BOIL

Frances Freeman
Arbuckle, California

2 large Cajun sausages, cut into
   $1^1/_2$ inch pieces
8 to 10 small red potatoes, unpeeled
1 tablespoon Old Bay seasoning
6 quarts water
2 to 3 lb. shelled, deveined uncooked
   medium shrimp
6 to 8 ears fresh corn, halved
$^1/_8$ teaspoon salt

1. In large pot, combine sausages, potatoes and Old Bay seasoning with enough water to cover; bring to a boil over medium heat. When potatoes are almost tender, add shrimp. When shrimp turn pink, add corn. Cover and cook until tender.

4 to 6 servings.

SPINACH TORTA

Kathleen Scarcelli Blair
Scottsdale, Arizona

1 (17.25-oz.) pkg. frozen puff pastry, thawed
5 eggs
2 (10-oz.) pkg. frozen chopped spinach, thawed, squeezed dry
2 cups (8 oz.) shredded mozzarella cheese
1 cup (4 oz.) ricotta cheese
1 (8-oz.) pkg. feta cheese, crumbled
3/4 cup (3 oz.) freshly grated Parmesan cheese
1/2 cup dry bread crumbs
1/4 cup chopped onion
1 (12-oz.) jar roasted red bell peppers, drained, sliced

1. Heat oven to 425°F. Spray 9-inch springform pan with nonstick cooking spray.

2. Roll 1 pastry sheet into 16-inch circle on lightly floured surface. Press into bottom and up sides of pan, leaving 2-inch overhang.

3. In large bowl, combine 4 of the eggs, spinach, cheeses, bread crumbs and onion; mix well. Spoon half the mixture into pan. Add layer of red peppers. Top with remaining half of mixture.

4. Roll remaining pastry sheet on lightly floured surface. Cut 9-inch circle and place over filling; pinch edges to seal.

5. Bake 40 minutes or until golden brown and filling is set. Cool 30 minutes. Run knife along edges and carefully remove from pan. Serve warm or at room temperature.

10 servings.

PEGGY'S PAELLA

Peggy Winkworth
Durango, Colorado

1/4 cup olive oil
1/4 cup finely chopped onion
2 garlic cloves, crushed
2 whole boneless skinless chicken breasts, cut into 1/2-inch pieces
2 cups long-grain rice
1 center cut slice ham, cut into 1/2-inch cubes
1/4 teaspoon ground saffron
4 cups reduced-sodium chicken broth
1 cup frozen peas, thawed
1 teaspoon salt
1/4 teaspoon freshly ground pepper
2 lb. shelled, deveined uncooked medium shrimp
24 fresh clams in shells, washed*
1 (14.5-oz.) can artichoke hearts, halved
1 (2.25-oz.) can sliced ripe olives

1. Heat oil in large skillet over medium-high heat until hot. Sauté onion, garlic and chicken until golden. Add rice and ham; sauté until rice is tender. Add saffron, broth, peas, salt and pepper; simmer, covered, 30 minutes or until rice is fluffy.

2. Add shrimp, clams, artichoke hearts and olives to skillet. Simmer, covered, an additional 15 to 20 minutes or until shrimp turn pink and clams open.

6 to 8 servings.

TIP *Clams that do not open when cooking are inedible and should be discarded.

SHRIMP NEWBURG

Charlotte Ward
Hilton Head Island, South Carolina

1 tablespoon kosher (coarse) salt
1 (8-oz.) pkg. egg noodles
1 tablespoon butter
1 lb. shelled, deveined uncooked
  medium shrimp
2 cups water
1 ($10^3/4$-oz.) can condensed cream
  of shrimp soup
1 (11-oz.) can evaporated milk
$1/2$ cup mayonnaise
$1/4$ cup (1-oz.) shredded sharp
  cheddar cheese
$1/4$ cup dry sherry

1. Heat oven to 350°F. Spray 3-quart casserole with nonstick cooking spray.

2. Fill large pot two-thirds full of water; add 1 table-spoon salt. Bring to a boil over medium-high heat. Cook egg noodles according to package directions. Rinse and drain thoroughly. Set aside.

3. In large skillet, heat butter over medium-high heat until melted. Add shrimp; sauté 2 minutes or until shrimp turn pink. Set aside.

4. In large bowl, combine soup and milk; mix well. Stir in mayonnaise, cheese, sherry, noodles and shrimp; mix well.

5. Pour mixture into casserole. Bake 30 minutes or until golden brown.

4 servings.

JAMBALAYA

Tammy Raynes
Natchitoches, Louisiana

$3/4$ cup chopped onion
$1/2$ cup chopped celery
$1/4$ cup chopped green bell pepper
2 garlic cloves, minced
2 tablespoons butter
2 cups cooked cubed ham
1 (28-oz.) can diced tomatoes
1 ($10^3/4$-oz.) can reduced-sodium
  beef broth
1 cup long-grain rice
1 cup water
1 teaspoon sugar
1 teaspoon dried thyme
$1/2$ teaspoon chili powder
$1/4$ teaspoon freshly ground pepper
$1^1/2$ lb. shelled, deveined uncooked
  medium shrimp
1 tablespoon chopped fresh parsley

1. In Dutch oven, sauté onion, celery, bell pepper and garlic in butter over medium-high heat until tender. Add ham, tomatoes, broth, rice, water, sugar, thyme, chili powder and pepper; bring to a boil.

2. Reduce heat; cover and simmer about 25 minutes or until rice is tender. Add shrimp and parsley; simmer, uncovered, 7 to 10 minutes or until shrimp turn pink.

8 servings.

Scallops & Asparagus in Champagne Risotto

SCALLOPS & ASPARAGUS IN CHAMPAGNE RISOTTO

Carol Bower
Meriden, Connecticut

3 tablespoons unsalted butter
1/4 lb. sliced mushrooms
1/4 cup chopped green onions
2 garlic cloves, finely chopped
2/3 cup Arborio or medium-grain
   white rice
1 cup dry Champagne
1 (14.5-oz.) can reduced-sodium
   chicken broth
1/2 lb. fresh asparagus, cut into 2-inch
   pieces
1/2 lb. bay scallops
1/4 cup (1 oz.) freshly grated
   Parmesan cheese
1/8 teaspoon salt
1/8 teaspoon freshly ground pepper

1. In large saucepan, melt butter over medium heat. Sauté mushrooms until tender. Remove from pan; keep warm.

2. Add green onions and garlic to skillet; sauté 2 minutes. Stir in rice; sauté 2 minutes. Stir in Champagne; simmer about 2 minutes or until almost all liquid evaporates, stirring frequently. Add broth; simmer 8 minutes, stirring frequently. Stir in asparagus. Simmer an additional 7 to 8 minutes or until rice is almost tender, stirring frequently. Add scallops; simmer about 5 minutes or until scallops are opaque, rice is tender but still firm and mixture is creamy. Stir in mushrooms and Parmesan; season with salt and pepper.

2 servings.

CASSEROLE OF BAKED CRAB IMPERIAL

David A. Heppner
Brandon, Florida

1 1/4 cups fresh bread crumbs
1 teaspoon butter plus 1/4 cup, melted
1/4 cup all-purpose flour
2 cups milk
1 teaspoon salt
1/2 teaspoon celery salt
1/8 teaspoon cayenne pepper
1/8 teaspoon freshly ground pepper
1 egg yolk, beaten
2 tablespoons sherry
1 lb. fresh crabmeat, drained
1 teaspoon minced fresh parsley
1 teaspoon minced onion
1/4 teaspoon paprika

1. Heat oven to 350°F. Spray 15x10x1-inch pan and 1 1/2-quart casserole with nonstick cooking spray.

2. In large bowl, combine 1/4 cup of the bread crumbs and 1 teaspoon of the butter; mix well. Spread buttered crumbs on pan; bake 3 to 5 minutes or until golden. Set aside. Increase heat to 400°F.

3. In large saucepan, melt remaining 1/4 cup butter over low heat. Stir in flour until smooth. Cook 1 minute, stirring constantly. Gradually add milk; increase heat to medium. Stir mixture constantly until thick and bubbly. Stir in salt, celery salt, cayenne pepper and black pepper.

4. In medium bowl, stir about one-fourth of the hot mixture into egg yolk; mix well. Add egg yolk mixture to remaining hot mixture. Remove saucepan from heat; add sherry, remaining 1 cup bread crumbs, crabmeat, parsley and onion. Stir gently.

5. Spoon into casserole. Top with buttered crumbs; sprinkle with paprika. Bake 20 to 25 minutes or until bubbly.

6 servings.

FLOUNDER STUFFED WITH SHRIMP

David A. Heppner
Brandon, Florida

1½ cups water
½ lb. deveined uncooked medium
  shrimp
½ cup butter, softened
1 (3-oz.) pkg. cream cheese, softened
½ cup (2 oz.) crumbled blue cheese
1 tablespoon fresh lemon juice
2 tablespoons minced onion
1½ teaspoons chopped fresh parsley
⅛ teaspoon freshly ground pepper
4 (6-oz.) flounder fillets
¼ cup dry white wine

1. Heat oven to 375°F. Spray 8-inch square pan with nonstick cooking spray.

2. In large pot, bring water to a boil over medium-high heat. Add shrimp; cook 3 to 5 minutes or until shrimp turn pink. Drain well; rinse shrimp under cold water. Peel shrimp; chop into 1-inch pieces.

3. In large bowl, combine shrimp, butter, cream cheese, blue cheese, lemon juice, onion, parsley and pepper; mix well.

4. Spread one-fourth of the shrimp mixture evenly over each fillet; roll up fillets and place seam side down in pan. Pour wine over fillets. Bake 20 minutes or until fish flakes easily with fork.

5. Place stuffed fillets on individual serving plates; spoon pan juices over fillets. Garnish with lemon twists, shrimp and fresh parsley sprigs.

4 servings.

CATFISH ETOUFEE (STEW)

Z. Burt Parker
Urbana, Illinois

1 (5-lb.) fish fillet, cut into 1-inch
  pieces
1 teaspoon salt
1 teaspoon freshly ground pepper
½ teaspoon cayenne pepper
3 tablespoons vegetable oil
2 garlic cloves, minced
1 bunch fresh parsley, chopped
1 large red bell pepper, chopped
3 ribs celery, chopped
1 bunch green onions, chopped
2 tablespoons all-purpose flour
1½ (8 oz.) cans tomato sauce
¼ teaspoon dried thyme
1 bay leaf
2 slices lemon
¼ cup water

1. Season fish with salt, black pepper and cayenne pepper.

2. In large pot, heat oil over low heat. Place half of the fish in pot. Remove pot from heat.

3. In large bowl, combine garlic, parsley, bell pepper, celery and onions; mix well. Toss half of the vegetables over fish. Sprinkle 1 tablespoon of the flour over vegetables. Top with half of the tomato sauce. Repeat layers.

4. Add thyme, bay leaf, lemon and water. Cook over low heat 1 hour or until fish flakes easily with fork. Do not stir. Discard bay leaf.

10 to 12 servings.

CHICKEN VERONIQUE

Ivan Huber
Boonton, New Jersey

4 (1-lb.) boneless skinless chicken
    breast halves, slightly pounded to
    even thickness
2 tablespoons fresh lemon juice
1/8 teaspoon salt
1/8 teaspoon freshly ground pepper
2 tablespoons all-purpose flour
1 tablespoon olive oil
1 tablespoon butter
1 tablespoon vegetable oil
$1/2$ cup reduced-sodium chicken broth
$1/3$ cup white wine or $1/4$ cup
    vermouth
1 cup seedless green grapes

1. Rinse chicken and pat dry.

2. Sprinkle lemon juice over chicken. Place chicken on rack and allow to dry at least 20 minutes. Season with salt and pepper. Lightly flour chicken, shaking off excess.

3. In large skillet, heat olive oil, butter and oil over medium-high heat until hot. Arrange chicken about 1 inch apart in skillet. (Cook in batches, if necessary.) Sauté chicken 5 to 10 minutes or until golden brown and juices run clear. Remove chicken from skillet; cover with aluminum foil.

4. Pour off excess fat. Deglaze pan with broth and wine. Boil 2 to 3 minutes, allowing alcohol to evaporate. If sauce is too thin, reduce by boiling a few minutes more. If too thick, add water. Reduce heat to medium. Add grapes; cover and cook 2 minutes. Add chicken to sauce; glaze 1 minute. Serve with grape garnish, rice and green salad, if desired.

4 servings.

CRANBERRY-BURGUNDY GLAZED HAM

David A. Heppner
Brandon, Florida

1 (10- to 14-lb.) bone-in cooked ham
Whole cloves
1 (16-oz.) can whole-berry cranberry
    sauce
$1/2$ cup packed brown sugar
$1/2$ cup dry red wine
1 tablespoon prepared mustard

1. Heat oven to 325°F.

2. Place ham, fat side up, on rack in shallow roasting pan. Score fat in diamond pattern; place clove in each diamond. Insert meat thermometer into thickest portion of ham without touching bone. Bake in oven about 3 hours or until thermometer registers 140°F.

3. Meanwhile, in medium saucepan, stir together cranberry sauce, brown sugar, wine and mustard; bring to a boil over medium heat. Reduce heat; simmer, uncovered, 5 minutes. Spoon half of sauce over ham during last 30 minutes of roasting. Reheat remaining sauce and pass with ham.

30 servings.

NEW MEXICO CHICKEN MOLE

David Lee Summer
Las Cruces, New Mexico

4 cups reduced-sodium chicken broth
5 dried ancho chiles
5 dried New Mexico red chile pods
1 tablespoon olive oil
1/2 lb. fresh Anaheim chiles, chopped
1 medium onion, chopped
1 green bell pepper, chopped
1/4 cup raisins
1 cup crushed tomatoes
1/2 cup pine nuts
1/2 cup pecans
1/4 cup sesame seeds
3/4 teaspoon cinnamon
1/2 teaspoon ground cloves
1/4 teaspoon ground cumin
6 tablespoons chopped unsweetened chocolate
2 tablespoons vegetable oil
6 boneless skinless chicken breast halves

1. In large pot, bring broth to a boil over medium-high heat. Stir in chiles and chile pods; reduce heat and simmer 30 minutes.

2. In large skillet, heat olive oil over medium-high heat until hot. Sauté Anaheim chiles, onion and bell pepper 2 to 3 minutes or until onion is browned. Add raisins and tomatoes; simmer 10 minutes.

3. Chop pine nuts, pecans and sesame seeds in blender. Combine broth and chile mixtures; blend until smooth. Add mixture to skillet. Stir in cinnamon, cloves and cumin. Simmer 10 minutes.

4. Meanwhile, combine chocolate and vegetable oil in medium bowl; mix together thoroughly. Add chocolate mixture to skillet.

5. In another large skillet, cook chicken over medium-high heat about 3 minutes per side until brown. Add chicken to sauce; simmer 15 to 30 minutes.

4 to 6 servings.

QUAILLES ROTIEN AUZ FRUIT SECS

(ROAST QUAIL WITH DRIED FRUIT STUFFING)

Gini Stoddard
Kapaa, Hawaii

16 (5-oz.) quails or 8 Cornish game hens
8 oz. dried apricots
4 oz. dried figs
1/4 cup raisins
4 oz. toasted hazelnuts*
1 tablespoon minced fresh mint
1/4 teaspoon salt
1/4 cup butter, softened
1/8 teaspoon freshly ground pepper

1. Heat oven to 400°F. Rinse quails and pat dry.

2. In large saucepan, combine apricots, figs and raisins with enough water to cover; bring to a boil over medium-high heat. Remove saucepan from heat. Let rest to soak up water.

3. Drain excess water from fruit. Chop fruit and combine with hazelnuts. Stir in mint and 1/8 teaspoon of the salt.

4. Stuff each quail with raisin mixture; truss with kitchen string. Rub birds with butter; season with remaining 1/8 teaspoon salt and pepper.

5. Bake, uncovered, 30 to 35 minutes or until internal temperature reaches 180°F.

8 servings.

TIP *To toast hazelnuts, bake at 375°F on baking sheet about 10 minutes or until lightly browned. Cool.

Roast Quail with Dried Fruit Stuffing

FANCY CHICKEN PUFF PIE

David A. Heppner
Brandon, Florida

¹/₄ cup butter
¹/₄ cup chopped shallots
¹/₄ cup all-purpose flour
1 cup reduced-sodium chicken broth
¹/₄ cup sherry
¹/₈ teaspoon salt
¹/₈ teaspoon ground white pepper
Dash ground nutmeg
¹/₄ lb. ham, cut into 2-x¹/₄-inch strips
3 cups cooked chicken, cut into
    2-x¹/₄-inch strips
1¹/₂ cups fresh or 1 (10-oz.) pkg.
    frozen asparagus, thawed
1 cup whipping cream
1 (9-inch) unbaked pie shell
1 egg, beaten

1. Heat oven to 425°F.

2. In medium saucepan, melt butter over medium-high heat; sauté shallots lightly. Stir in flour; cook 3 minutes. Stir in broth and sherry; heat to a boil, stirring constantly. Season with salt, pepper and nutmeg. Reduce heat to low and simmer 5 minutes. Stir in ham, chicken, asparagus and cream. Pour chicken mixture into 9-inch pie plate.

3. Cut 8-inch round from pastry shell. Cut hearts from extra dough with cookie cutter, if desired. Place round on cookie sheet moistened with cold water. Pierce with fork, decorate with hearts and brush with egg.

4. Place cookie sheet and pie plate in oven. Bake 10 minutes; reduce heat to 350°F. Bake an additional 10 to 15 minutes or until pastry is golden brown and filling is hot and set. With spatula, place pastry over hot filling. Serve immediately.

4 servings.

ROASTED CORNISH HENS WITH LEMON AND ROSEMARY

Lisa M. Alvares
Fayetteville, North Carolina

4 Cornish game hens, giblets removed
¹/₈ teaspoon salt
¹/₈ teaspoon freshly ground pepper
1 large lemon, peeled, juice reserved,
    cut into matchstick-size pieces
4 large garlic cloves, halved
4 sprigs fresh parsley
4 teaspoons fresh rosemary or
    2 teaspoons dried
3 tablespoons olive oil
¹/₂ to ³/₄ cup reduced-sodium chicken
    broth
¹/₃ cup dry white wine
3 tablespoons butter

1. Heat oven to 375°F. Spray large roasting pan with nonstick cooking spray.

2. Rinse hens and pat dry. Season cavities with salt and pepper. Divide lemon pieces equally in cavities with garlic, parsley and rosemary.

3. Gently lift skin away from breast meat by slipping fingers in between. Divide lemon strips among hens and place under skin. Fold wingtips under hens; secure legs.

4. Place hens in pan, breast side up. Brush generously with olive oil on all sides. Season with salt and pepper, if desired. Bake, basting every 15 minutes with broth, 50 to 60 minutes or until internal temperature reaches 180°F. Remove hens; set aside on warm platter.

5. Skim fat from pan juices. Place roasting pan over medium heat; stir in remaining broth and wine. Simmer and deglaze 15 minutes or until liquid reduces to about ¹/₂ cup. Stir in reserved lemon juice; whisk in butter a little at a time. Serve sauce over hens or separately. Garnish with parsley or fresh rosemary.

4 servings.

CHICKEN BREASTS DELUXE

Susan M. Bork
Indianapolis, Indiana

6 (about 1¹/₂ lb.) boneless skinless
   chicken breast halves
1 (10³/₄-oz.) can condensed cream of
   chicken soup
1 (10³/₄-oz.) can condensed cream of
   celery soup
¹/₂ cup cooking sherry
1 cup (4 oz.) shredded sharp cheddar
   cheese
4 green onions, thinly sliced

1. Heat oven to 300°F. Spray 2-quart casserole with nonstick cooking spray.

2. Arrange chicken in casserole.

3. In large bowl, combine soups and sherry; mix well. Stir in cheese and green onions. Pour mixture over chicken. Bake, uncovered, 1¹/₂ hours. Let stand 10 minutes before serving.

6 servings.

JENN'S YUMMY CHICKEN ENCHILADAS

Jennifer Lee Smith Mota
Provo, Utah

2 teaspoons butter
1 medium onion, diced
2 to 3 garlic cloves, minced
2¹/₂ lb. boneless skinless chicken
   breasts, cut into 1-inch pieces
¹/₈ teaspoon salt
¹/₈ teaspoon freshly ground pepper
1 (24-oz.) container sour cream
7¹/₃ cups (29 oz.) shredded Colby
   Jack cheese
2 (10³/₄-oz.) cans condensed cream
   of chicken soup
16 (8-inch) flour tortillas
2 (4-oz.) cans diced green chiles
2 (2.25-oz.) cans sliced ripe olives

1. Heat oven to 350°F. Spray 2 (2-quart) casseroles with nonstick cooking spray.

2. In large skillet, melt butter over medium-high heat. Sauté onion and garlic until onions are tender. Stir in chicken; cook until chicken is no longer pink in center. Season with salt and pepper. Place chicken in large bowl. Cool in refrigerator about 15 minutes. Add 2 cups of the sour cream and 4 cups of the cheese; stir until mixed.

3. In another large bowl, combine soup and remaining ³/₄ cup sour cream. Stir until thoroughly mixed. Spread ³/₄ cup of the soup mixture on bottom of each casserole. Warm tortillas in microwave at high power 10 to 15 seconds. Place ¹/₃ cup chicken mixture in center of each tortilla. Fold opposite sides of tortilla toward middle and roll from open end, enclosing mixture in middle. Continue with each tortilla.

4. Place 8 enchiladas in each casserole. Spread with remaining soup mixture. Top with chiles; sprinkle with remaining cheese. Bake, uncovered, about 45 minutes or until enchiladas are hot. Top with olives. Serve with a dollop of guacamole and salsa, if desired.

8 to 10 servings.

Macadamia Nut & Gorgonzola Chicken Wellington

MACADAMIA NUT & GORGONZOLA CHICKEN WELLINGTON

Gini Stoddard
Kapaa, Hawaii

2 tablespoons Gorgonzola or blue
  cheese, room temperature
2 tablespoons reduced-fat cream
  cheese, softened
1 1/2 teaspoons cognac, dry sherry or
  fresh orange juice
2 tablespoons minced fresh parsley
1/8 teaspoon freshly ground pepper
2/3 cup coarsely chopped macadamia
  nuts
1 egg, separated
1 teaspoon milk or water
1 large boneless skinless chicken
  breast
2 tablespoons butter
1 (17.25-oz.) pkg. frozen puff pastry,
  thawed
Raspberry and Plum Wine Sauce
  (page 25)

1. Line 15x10x1-inch pan with parchment paper.

2. In small bowl, combine Gorgonzola and cream cheese. Stir in cognac, parsley and pepper; mix well. (If mixture is too thick add a few drops of cream or milk; mixture should be thick enough to stay on chicken.)

3. In small skillet, toast nuts over medium-high heat, shaking pan frequently. Toast until slightly golden, being careful not to scorch. Set aside.

4. In small bowl, whisk egg white until just frothy. Stir in milk. Set aside. In another small bowl, beat egg yolk. Set aside.

5. Pound chicken breast; spread each breast with cream cheese mixture. Sprinkle with nuts. Roll up; secure with wooden toothpicks. Sauté chicken in butter over medium heat in large skillet.

6. Roll out 1 piece of pastry on lightly floured board to measure 16x16 inches. Cut into 4 (8-x8-inch) squares. Brush 1 pastry strip with egg white mixture.

7. Allow sautéed chicken bundles to cool 10 minutes; remove toothpicks. Wrap in pastry, making sure seam is at bottom of chicken bundle.

8. Brush top and sides of pastry with beaten egg yolk. Cut excess pastry into leaf patterns and place on top; brush with yolk mixture. Dust leaves slightly with paprika, if desired. Repeat with remaining pastry, chicken, cheese and nuts.

9. Heat oven to 400°F. Bake 20 to 25 minutes or until pastry is golden.

2 servings.

FESTIVE ROAST PORK

David A. Heppner
Brandon, Florida

1 (5-lb.) boneless pork loin roast,
  rolled, tied
$3/4$ cup dry red wine
$1/3$ cup packed brown sugar
$1/4$ cup vinegar
$1/4$ cup ketchup
$1/4$ cup water
2 tablespoons vegetable oil
1 tablespoon low-sodium soy sauce
1 garlic clove, minced
1 teaspoon curry powder
$1/2$ teaspoon ground ginger
$1/4$ teaspoon freshly ground pepper
2 teaspoons cornstarch

1. Place roast in large plastic resealable bag; set in large, deep bowl. For marinade, combine wine, brown sugar, vinegar, ketchup, water, oil, soy sauce, garlic, curry, ginger and pepper in small bowl; mix well. Pour marinade over meat; seal bag. Marinate in refrigerator 6 to 8 hours or overnight, turning bag several times. Drain meat, reserving $1 1/4$ cups marinade. Pat meat dry with paper towels.

2. Heat oven to 325°F. Place meat on rack in shallow roasting pan. Insert meat thermometer. Bake about $2 1/4$ to $2 1/2$ hours or until thermometer registers 160°F.

3. About 25 minutes before meat is thoroughly cooked, prepare sauce. In small saucepan, stir cornstarch into reserved marinade. Cook and stir until thickened and bubbly. Cook an additional 2 minutes. Brush roast frequently with sauce during last 15 minutes of baking.

4. Let meat stand, covered, about 15 minutes before slicing. Meat temperature will rise about 5°F while standing. Reheat remaining sauce and pass with meat.

15 servings.

TURKEY WITH SAUSAGE-PECAN STUFFING

David A. Heppner
Brandon, Florida

4 medium onions
1 lb. bulk pork sausage
2 (6-oz.) pkg. herb stuffing mix
1 (15-oz.) pkg. golden raisins
1 cup sliced pecans
6 ribs celery, diced
$1/4$ teaspoon dried basil
$1/4$ teaspoon dried oregano
$1/4$ teaspoon curry powder
$1/4$ teaspoon caraway seeds
$1/4$ teaspoon poultry seasoning
$1/4$ teaspoon garlic powder
$1/4$ teaspoon salt
$1/4$ teaspoon freshly ground pepper
$2 1/2$ cups reduced-sodium chicken
  broth
1 (12- to 14-lb.) turkey

1. Heat oven to 325°F. Spray 2 ($1 1/2$-quart) casseroles with nonstick cooking spray.

2. Slice 2 of the onions; set aside. Chop remaining 2 onions.

3. In large skillet, cook sausage and chopped onion over medium heat until sausage is no longer pink in center; add herb packet from stuffing mixes. Stir in raisins, pecans, celery and seasonings; simmer 10 minutes. Add stuffing mixes and broth; stir well. Cook and stir 5 minutes.

4. Place sliced onion inside turkey. Add 6 to 7 cups stuffing. Place remaining stuffing in casserole; cover and refrigerate. Skewer openings; secure drumsticks. Place on rack in roasting pan.

5. Bake, uncovered, 4 to $4 1/2$ hours or internal temperature reaches 180°F. Baste often with shortening. When turkey begins to brown, baste if needed and cover lightly with aluminum foil.

6. During last hour of baking turkey, place reserved stuffing in second casserole. Bake covered, 1 hour. Uncover and bake an additional 10 minutes.

12 to 14 servings.

ARMENIAN DOLMA IN CABBAGE LEAVES

Dzhangirova A. Svetlana
Seattle, Washington

1 cup chopped onion
1 lb. ground lamb
$1/2$ cup cooked rice
1 tablespoon finely chopped fresh
   cilantro
1 tablespoon finely chopped fresh
   basil
1 tablespoon finely chopped fresh
   marjoram or oregano
$1/8$ teaspoon salt
$1/8$ teaspoon freshly ground pepper
1 ($1^1/2$ lb.) head cabbage, cored
   (12 large leaves)
1 large quince, sliced
$1/2$ cup dried apricot halves
$1/4$ cup butter
3 tablespoons tomato paste
$1/2$ teaspoon salt
1 cup hot water

1. Heat oven to 350°F. Spray 3-quart casserole with nonstick cooking spray.

2. In large mixing bowl combine $1/2$ cup of the chopped onion, lamb, rice, herbs, salt and pepper. Set aside.

3. In large pot, boil cabbage 10 minutes or until outer leaves are tender; drain. Remove outer leaves; cut out thick vein for easier rolling. Place spoonful of lamb mixture on each leaf; fold in sides. Arrange seam-side down into casserole; arrange sliced quince and apricots between cabbage dolma (rolls).

4. In large skillet, melt butter over medium heat. Add remaining $1/2$ cup chopped onion; sauté until onion is tender. Stir in tomato paste, salt and hot water; simmer 10 minutes, stirring occasionally.

5. Pour tomato sauce over top of dolma to cover. Cover pan with lid or aluminum foil; cook over medium-high heat 1 hour on until lamb is no longer pink in center. Serve cabbage rolls on large plate. Arrange quice and apricots around rolls. Pour pan juices over.

4 servings.

CREOLE STUFFING

Tammy Raynes
Natchitoches, Louisiana

4 cups cubed cornbread
2 cups cubed dried whole wheat
   bread, crusts removed
1 cup cooked chopped ham
$3/4$ cup chopped smoked kielbasa
$1/2$ cup chopped red bell pepper
$1/4$ cup chopped celery
3 tablespoons chopped onion
$2^1/2$ teaspoons Creole seasoning
2 eggs, lightly beaten
$1^1/2$ cups reduced-sodium chicken
   broth

1. Heat oven to 325°F. Spray 2-quart casserole with nonstick cooking spray.

2. In large bowl, combine cornbread, bread cubes, ham, kielbasa, bell pepper, celery, onion, Creole seasoning and eggs; mix well. Stir in broth; mix well.

3. Transfer mixture to casserole. Cover and bake 60 minutes. Uncover and bake an additional 10 minutes or until lightly browned.

6 to 8 servings.

MARINATED BEEF FOR 10 OR MORE

Gini Stoddard
Kapaa, Hawaii

1 (5-lb.) beef rolled rump roast
1/4 cup apple cider vinegar
1 1/2 cups water
1/2 cup sugar
4 teaspoons Dijon mustard
1/2 cup ketchup
1/4 teaspoon cayenne pepper
1/4 teaspoon freshly ground pepper
1 teaspoon salt
1 tablespoon Worcestershire sauce
1/4 cup low-sodium soy sauce
2 medium onions, sliced
2 garlic cloves, minced
2 slices lemon (1 inch thick)
1/4 cup red wine, if desired

1. Heat oven to 325°F. Bake roast 3 hours or until internal temperature reaches at least 140°F. Cool and thinly slice.

2. Meanwhile, bring vinegar, water, sugar, mustard, ketchup, cayenne pepper, black pepper, salt, Worcestershire sauce, wine, soy sauce, onions, garlic and lemon slice to a boil in large saucepan over medium heat.

3. Place meat slices in 3-quart casserole, overlapping diagonally. Pour hot marinade over meat, making sure sauce gets between slices. Cover with aluminum foil and refrigerate 24 hours. Bake covered, 1 hour or until internal temperature reaches 160°F.

15 servings.

SAUSAGE STUFFED PORK ROAST

Vivian Nikanow
Chicago, Illinois

ROAST
1 (4-lb.) pork loin rib roast
1 lb. bulk pork sausage
1/2 cup chopped onion
1 garlic clove, minced
2 eggs, slightly beaten
1 3/4 cup herb-seasoned stuffing mix
1/4 cup (1-oz.) freshly grated
    Parmesan cheese
1 (7.5-oz.) can spinach, drained,
    chopped
2 to 4 tablespoons reduced-sodium
    chicken broth

GRAVY
1/4 cup reduced-sodium chicken broth,
    plus more if needed
1/2 cup water
3 tablespoons all-purpose flour
1/2 teaspoon dried basil
1/8 teaspoon each salt, freshly ground
    pepper

1. Heat oven to 325°F. Cut 6 pockets in roast corresponding to 6 ribs. In large skillet, cook sausage, onion and garlic over medium heat until sausage is no longer pink in center; drain. In large bowl, combine eggs, stuffing mix, cheese and spinach. Stir in meat mixture and broth.

2. Stuff about 1/3 cup mixture into each pocket. Place roast, fat side up, in open roasting pan. Bake 2 to 2 1/2 hours, covering loosely with aluminum foil after f irst hour, until internal temperature reaches 170°F. Heat remaining stuffing in covered 1 1/2-quart casserole during last 30 minutes baking time.

3. To make gravy, pour meat juices from roasting pan into measuring cup. Add 1/4 cup broth to pan; deglaze. Pour mixture into measuring cup; add enough broth to equal 2 cups liquid. Pour into saucepan. Combine water with flour; stir into saucepan. Season with basil, salt and pepper. Cook and stir until thickened and bubbly. Serve with roast.

6 servings.

Sausage Stuffed Pork Roast

HERBED POULTRY WITH SPINACH STUFFING

Vivian Nikanow
Chicago, Illinois

1 (5- to 6-lb.) whole roasting chicken
1 tablespoon olive oil
1 teaspoon crushed dried basil
1 teaspoon crushed dried oregano
1 teaspoon crushed dried parsley
$1/4$ teaspoon garlic salt
2 (10-oz.) pkg. frozen chopped
  spinach, thawed, squeezed dry
1 cup finely chopped mixed red and
  green bell peppers
4 oz. proscuitto ham chopped
$3/4$ cup fresh bread crumbs
$1/2$ cup sliced green onion
$1/3$ cup pine nuts or slivered almonds
$1/4$ cup butter, melted
$1/4$ teaspoon freshly ground pepper
Dash nutmeg

1. Heat oven to 325°F.

2. Rinse chicken and pat dry. Brush with olive oil. In small bowl, combine basil, oregano, parsley and garlic salt; mix well. Sprinkle mixture over chicken and rub in. Cover and refrigerate up to 24 hours. In large mixing bowl, combine spinach, bell peppers, prosciutto, bread crumbs, onions, nuts, butter, pepper and nutmeg; mix well. Cover and refrigerate up to 24 hours.

3. Slip fingers between chicken skin and breast, forming pocket. Press $1/4$ of the stuffing loosely into pocket and also into neck cavity. Pull neck skin to back; fasten with small skewer. Lightly spoon remaining stuffing into body cavity. Tuck drumsticks under band of skin that crosses tail. If there is no band, tie drumsticks to tail. Twist wing tips under back.

4. Place stuffed chicken, breast side up, on rack in shallow roasting pan. Bake, uncovered, 2 to $2^1/2$ hours or until thermometer reads 180°F. After $1^1/2$ hours, cut band of skin or string between drumsticks so that thighs cook evenly. Remove chicken and cover with aluminum foil. Let stand 10 to 20 minutes before carving.

10 servings.

POPOVER WITH HOT TURKEY SALAD

Nancy West
Aurora, Illinois

2 eggs, room temperature
$1^1/4$ cups milk, room temperature
1 cup all-purpose flour
$1/2$ teaspoon salt
4 cups cooked diced turkey
2 cups diced celery
2 cups (8 oz.) shredded cheddar
  cheese
1 (2.25-oz.) can sliced ripe olives,
  drained
1 cup mayonnaise
$1/8$ teaspoon freshly ground pepper
Pinch onion powder
$1^1/2$ cups crushed potato chips

1. Heat oven to 400°F. Spray 9-inch pie plate with nonstick cooking spray.

2. In large bowl, beat eggs at medium speed until frothy; add 1 cup of the milk, flour and salt. Beat mixture just until smooth; pour into pie plate. Bake 35 to 40 minutes or until deep golden brown. Immediately prick with fork in center to steam.

3. In large saucepan, combine turkey, celery, cheese, olives, mayonnaise, remaining $1/4$ cup milk, pepper and onion powder; cook and stir over low heat until heated through. Stir in potato chips.

4. Spoon mixture over popover. Garnish with tomato wedges. Serve immediately.

8 servings.

NOTE This dish is great after Thanksgiving with turkey leftovers. But I also make it year-round, and the comments are endless.

ORANGE-GLAZED ROAST DUCKLING WITH APPLE STUFFING

David A. Heppner–Brandon, Florida

1 (5-lb.) duck, dressed
1 teaspoon caraway seeds
¼ cup plus 2 tablespoons butter
1 small onion, chopped
4 cups peeled chopped apples
3 cups fresh bread crumbs
1 cup chopped celery
¼ cup raisins
2 tablespoons minced fresh parsley
1 teaspoon salt
2 teaspoons freshly ground pepper
½ teaspoon paprika
¼ teaspoon ground cloves
1 cup water
½ cup packed brown sugar
2½ tablespoons sugar
1 tablespoon cornstarch
1 tablespoon grated orange peel
1 cup fresh orange juice
Dash hot pepper sauce

1. Heat oven to 350°F.

2. Remove giblets and neck from duck; reserve for another use. Rinse duck and pat dry. Sprinkle cavity with caraway seeds. In large skillet, melt butter over medium-high heat. Sauté onion, stirring constantly until tender.

3. In large bowl, combine onion, apples, bread crumbs, celery, raisins, parsley, salt, pepper, paprika, cloves and water; stir well. Spoon mixture into cavity; close with skewers. Secure legs together with string. Lift wingtips up and over back and tuck under bird. Place duck on rack in shallow roasting pan, breast side up. Insert meat thermometer into meaty portion of thigh. Bake, uncovered, 1½ hours.

4. In small saucepan, combine brown sugar, sugar, cornstarch, orange peel, orange juice and hot pepper sauce; bring to a boil. Reduce heat and cook, uncovered, 5 minutes, stirring occasionally. Bake duck an additional 30 minutes or until internal temperature reaches 180°F. Baste frequently with orange juice mixture. Remove to serving platter; let stand 10 minutes before carving.

4 servings.

RASPBERRY AND PLUM WINE SAUCE

Gini Stoddard–Kapaa, Hawaii

1 cup frozen raspberries or cherries
1 cup imported Japanese plum wine
1 tablespoon balsamic vinegar
1 tablespoon grated orange peel

1. Bring raspberries and wine to a boil in small saucepan. Reduce heat and simmer, uncovered, about 15 minutes or until wine is reduced by half. Remove from heat; cool.

2. Press raspberries through fine sieve over small bowl. If using cherries, puree before straining. Add vinegar and orange peel. Stir and taste, adjusting if necessary. Add 1 teaspoon honey for sweeter taste. Return to saucepan and reheat, or refrigerate until ready to use.

2 servings.

Tenderloin of Beef

TENDERLOIN OF BEEF

David A. Heppner
Brandon, Florida

¹/₄ cup extra-virgin olive oil
10 cups chopped fresh spinach
2 tablespoons goat cheese
¹/₂ teaspoon fresh lemon juice
³/₄ teaspoon kosher (coarse) salt
3 tablespoons butter
1 cup minced shallots
4 cups assorted fresh mushrooms
2 tablespoons minced garlic
³/₄ cup dry marsala wine
¹/₈ teaspoon cayenne pepper
¹/₂ cup dry bread crumbs
1 (3- to 3¹/₂-lb.) beef tenderloin,
  center cut
8 thin slices prosciutto
1 teaspoon freshly ground pepper

1. Heat oven to 450°F.

2. In large skillet, heat oil over medium-high heat until hot. Increase heat to high. In batches, sauté spinach, turning quickly until wilted. Drain and press spinach in colander; coarsely chop. In large bowl, combine spinach with goat cheese, lemon juice and ¹/₄ teaspoon of the salt; refrigerate.

3. In same skillet, melt butter over low heat; sauté shallots until golden. Add mushrooms and garlic; sauté until just softened. Increase heat to medium-high; add wine. Reduce until wine is almost gone. Season with remaining ¹/₂ teaspoon salt and cayenne pepper. In food processor, pulse mushroom mixture and bread crumbs until crumbled. Refrigerate mixture.

4. Remove silver skin from tenderloin; remove excess fat. Make long cut down center of tenderloin to within 1 inch of bottom. (Do not cut all the way through. It's best to do this with several shallow cuts.) Repeat along two sides created, making four rows of meat all connected at bottom. Cover tenderloin with plastic wrap. With flat side of mallet, gently pound meat to between ¹/₂ to ³/₄ inches thick. Remove plastic wrap. Season tenderloin with salt and pepper.

5. Spread with thin layers of spinach filling, keeping it 1 to 1¹/₂ inches from edge. Add 1 layer proscuitto. Add layer of mushroom filling, being careful not to pack mixture down.

6. Fold each short side over filling, just far enough to hold. Tenderloin should now form rectangle. Using entire surface of both hands, roll up tenderloin, making sure sides stay tucked in. Place seam side down. Cut 12 (16-inch) pieces cotton string. Starting in center and working to ends, slide one piece string under meat and secure, spacing strings about 1 inch apart. Once secure, clip string ends.

7. Brush meat lightly with olive oil. Sprinkle pepper on parchment paper. Place meat on paper's edge and roll up; remove paper. Place meat, seam side down, in greased roasting pan. Bake until internal temperature reaches at least 160°F. Remove from oven; let rest 10 minutes wrapped in aluminum foil to hold temperature. When ready to serve, carve ³/₄-inch slices. Serve with rich brown sauce under meat, if desired.

12 servings.

CANNELLONI

Vivian Nikanow
Chicago, Illinois

CREPES
2½ cups milk
2 eggs
2 egg yolks
2 tablespoons unsalted butter, melted
½ teaspoon salt
2 cups all-purpose flour, sifted

FILLING
2 lb. ricotta cheese
2 (10-oz.) pkg. frozen chopped
   spinach, thawed, squeezed dry
¼ cup finely chopped Italian
   proscuitto or baked ham
Dash nutmeg
⅛ teaspoon salt
⅛ teaspoon freshly ground pepper
⅛ teaspoon freshly grated Parmesan
   cheese

BÉCHAMEL SAUCE
4 tablespoons butter
4 tablespoons all-purpose flour
1½ cups milk
⅛ teaspoon salt
Dash nutmeg
Dash freshly ground pepper

1. Spray medium skillet with nonstick cooking spray. In medium bowl, combine milk, eggs, egg yolks, butter, salt and flour; mix well. Pour about half of the mixture into skillet. Cook over medium-low heat until set; flip and cook other side. Do not let crepes brown. Place cooked crepes on plate; set aside. In another medium bowl, combine ricotta, spinach, proscuitto, nutmeg, salt, pepper and Parmesan cheese; mix well. Place 2 tablespoons filling in center of each crepe; roll up. Arrange crepes seam side down in 3-quart casserole. Set aside.

2. In small skillet, melt butter over medium heat; stir in flour. Reduce heat; cook 1 minute. Gradually add milk, stirring constantly. Increase heat to medium; cook 2 minutes or until sauce has thickened. Pour sauce over prepared crepes. Bake 30 to 45 minutes or until crepes are heated through and golden brown.

12 servings.

SUNDAY FARMHOUSE ROAST PORK

Deanna Jones
Parker, Colorado

1 (4-lb.) boneless pork loin roast
3 large garlic cloves, slivered
¼ cup unsalted butter, softened
2 tablespoons Dijon mustard
1 tablespoon chopped fresh thyme or
   1 teaspoon dried
½ teaspoon freshly ground pepper
1 cup reduced-sodium chicken broth
¾ cup dry white wine
1 tablespoon apricot jam or preserves

1. Heat oven to 350°F.

2. Cut slits into pork loin; insert garlic slivers. Place pork in shallow roasting pan; set aside.

3. In small bowl, mix together butter, mustard, thyme and pepper. Spread evenly over pork.

4. In medium saucepan, heat broth, wine and jam until jam dissolves; pour mixture over pork.

5. Bake pork on center rack of oven until internal temperature reaches 160°F, about 1½ hours or 20 minutes per pound. Baste frequently, adding a bit more wine if necessary. Let pork stand 15 minutes before slicing.

12 servings.

SIZZLING GRILLING

THAI-STYLE GRILLED SHRIMP WITH MANGO SALSA

Shirley Desantis
Bethlehem, Pennsylvania

SAUCE
1/3 cup creamy peanut butter
1/3 cup low-sodium soy sauce
1/4 cup honey
2 tablespoons extra-virgin olive oil
1 1/2 tablespoons water
3 garlic cloves, minced
1 1/2 teaspoons finely chopped fresh
    ginger

SALSA
2 medium mangoes, coarsely chopped
1/2 cup chopped fresh cilantro
1/3 cup chopped red onion
1/4 cup fresh lime juice
2 or 3 chipotle chiles in adobo sauce,
    chopped*

SHRIMP
2 lb. shelled, deveined uncooked
    medium shrimp
1 medium red onion, cut into 1-inch
    pieces
3 cups hot cooked rice
1/4 cup coarsely chopped roasted
    peanuts
1/4 cup chopped fresh cilantro

1. Place peanut butter in medium saucepan. Slowly whisk in soy sauce, honey, oil, water, garlic and ginger. Bring to a boil over medium heat. Reduce heat to low; simmer 10 minutes. (Sauce can be made up to 1 day ahead. Cover and refrigerate. Reheat over medium heat before using.) Reserve 1/3 cup sauce to brush on shrimp and onion after grilling.

2. In medium bowl, stir together mangoes, cilantro, onion, lime juice and chiles. (Salsa can be made up to 3 hours ahead. Cover and refrigerate. Remove from refrigerator about 15 minutes before serving.)

3. Heat grill. Thread shrimp alternately with onion on 8 (10- to 12-inch) metal skewers. Brush shrimp and onion with peanut sauce; place on gas grill over medium heat or on charcoal grill 4 to 6 inches from medium coals. Cook 5 to 6 minutes or until shrimp turn pink, turning once. Brush with reserved 1/3 cup peanut sauce.

4. Serve shrimp and onion over rice; sprinkle with peanuts and cilantro. Accompany with salsa.

8 servings.

TIP *Chipotle chiles in adobo sauce can be found in the Hispanic foods section of most supermarkets. If desired, remove some or all of the seeds. Any remaining chipotle chiles can be covered and refrigerated about 1 week or frozen up to 3 months.

Thai-Style Grilled Shrimp with Mango Salsa

GRILLED SALMON SUPREME

Florence Bogstad
Northridge, California

1 1/2 cups water
1 cup packed brown sugar
1/4 cup kosher (coarse) salt
1 tablespoon grated fresh ginger
2 bay leaves
2 teaspoons crushed allspice*
1 (3-lb.) salmon fillet (1 inch thick)
1 tablespoon honey

1. In medium saucepan, bring water, brown sugar, salt, ginger, bay leaves and allspice to a boil over medium-high heat, stirring occasionally. Remove from heat; cool.

2. Place salmon, skin side down, in large resealable plastic bag or nonreactive pan. Pour brine over salmon. Seal bag or cover pan with plastic wrap. Refrigerate 4 to 6 hours, spooning brine over salmon occasionally.

3. Heat grill. Soak 1 1/2 cups wood chips, such as hickory or oak chips, in warm water at least 15 minutes. Drain; place in chip container or on foil. Place in grill.

4. Rinse brine from salmon; pat dry with paper towels. Cut piece of foil twice the size of the salmon; fold foil in half lengthwise. Place salmon on foil skin side down; cut foil around salmon with scissors, leaving at least 1-inch rim around salmon. Brush salmon with honey.

5. Place salmon with foil on gas grill over low heat or on charcoal grill 4 to 6 inches from low coals. Cook 25 to 30 minutes or until fish just begins to flake, turning once..

8 servings.

TIP *Place allspice in plastic bag; crush with flat side of meat mallet or with rolling pin.

MAPLE-GLAZED TURKEY TENDERLOIN

Jamie Babb
Newbury, Ohio

2 (1 1/4 lb.) turkey tenderloins
1 teaspoon grated lemon peel
1/4 cup fresh lemon juice
2 tablespoons high-quality whiskey
1 cup pure maple syrup
1/3 cup extra-virgin olive oil
1/4 cup butter
2 tablespoons packed brown sugar

1. Rinse turkey and pat dry.

2. Place turkey in resealable plastic bag. In small bowl, combine lemon peel, lemon juice, whiskey, 1/2 cup of the syrup and oil; mix well. Reserve 1/3 cup; pour remaining marinade over turkey. Seal bag; refrigerate 4 hours, turning occasionally.

3. Pour reserved marinade in small saucepan; add remaining 1/2 cup syrup, butter and brown sugar. Heat to a boil; simmer 3 to 4 minutes.

4. Remove turkey from marinade; discard marinade. Place turkey on gas grill over medium heat or on charcoal grill 4 to 6 inches from medium coals. Cook 20 to 30 minutes, basting with sauce and turning every 7 to 8 minutes until no longer pink in center.

4 to 6 servings.

ORANGE GRILLED CHICKEN WITH PECAN-ORANGE COUSCOUS

Terry Ann Moore—Oaklyn, New Jersey

MARINADE
6 (1¹/₂ lb.) boneless skinless chicken
   breast halves
2 tablespoons orange marmalade
3 tablespoons sesame seeds
3 tablespoons frozen orange juice
   concentrate, thawed
2 tablespoons low-sodium soy sauce
2 tablespoons sesame oil
1 teaspoon grated orange peel
1 teaspoon grated lemon peel
¹/₄ teaspoon salt
¹/₄ teaspoon freshly ground pepper
4 green onions, sliced
2 garlic cloves, minced

COUSCOUS
2 (5.8-oz.) pkg. couscous
2¹/₂ cups fresh orange juice
¹/₄ cup chopped pecans, toasted*
¹/₄ cup sliced green onions
1 teaspoon grated orange peel

GARNISH
¹/₂ cup finely chopped pecans, toasted*
¹/₄ cup sliced green onions
Long strands of peel from 1 orange
   and 1 lemon

1. Place chicken in large resealable plastic bag. Place marmalade in small microwave-safe cup; microwave on high 20 seconds or until warm. In medium bowl, whisk together warm marmalade, sesame seeds, orange juice, soy sauce, sesame oil, orange peel, lemon peel, salt, pepper, green onions and garlic. Pour over chicken. Seal bag; refrigerate 2 to 3 hours.

2. Heat grill. Prepare couscous according to package directions, using 2¹/₂ cups orange juice in place of the water. Right before serving, stir in ¹/₄ cup pecans, ¹/₄ cup green onions and 1 teaspoon orange peel.

3. When ready to grill, remove chicken from marinade; discard marinade. Place chicken on gas grill over medium heat or on charcoal grill 4 to 6 inches from medium coals. Cook 10 to 12 minutes or until juices run clear, turning once. Serve chicken over couscous. Garnish with pecans, green onions and strands of orange and lemon peel.

6 servings.

TIP *To toast nuts, spread on baking sheet; bake at 375°F 7 to 10 minutes or until lightly browned. Cool.

COFFEE-FLAVORED BBQ RIBS

Cathy Cutler—Lubbock, Texas

5 lb. baby back pork ribs
3 tablespoons hot pepper sauce
1 large white onion, minced
¹/₄ cup Worcestershire sauce
²/₃ cup ketchup
¹/₄ cup brewed coffee
¹/₄ cup packed brown sugar
¹/₄ cup corn oil
2 tablespoons cider vinegar
1 teaspoon each chili powder, ground
   cumin, salt
¹/₂ teaspoon dry mustard

1. Heat grill. Rub ribs with hot pepper sauce. In medium saucepan, bring onion, Worcestershire sauce, ketchup, coffee, brown sugar, oil, vinegar, chili powder, cumin, salt and dry mustard to a boil; reduce heat and simmer 10 minutes.

2. Pour half the sauce over ribs. Grill ribs over medium heat or 4 to 6 inches from medium coals. Cook 25 minutes per side or until slightly pink in center. Baste occasionally.

10 servings.

Cuban Grilled Pork on a Bed of Gazpacho

CUBAN GRILLED PORK ON A BED OF GAZPACHO

Ann Noble Chupita
New Brighton, Minnesota

MARINADE
1 ($^3/_4$- to 1-lb.) pork tenderloin, cut into 4 pieces
3 tablespoons fresh lime juice
3 tablespoons water
2 tablespoons minced fresh cilantro
1 tablespoon minced jalapeño chile
$^3/_4$ teaspoon seasoned salt
1 teaspoon minced fresh garlic
$^1/_4$ teaspoon ground cumin
$^1/_4$ teaspoon freshly ground pepper

GAZPACHO
1 red bell pepper, coarsely chopped
1 yellow bell pepper, coarsely chopped
1 cucumber, peeled, coarsely chopped
$^1/_2$ small red onion or 3 green onions, coarsely chopped
$^1/_2$ small jicama, peeled, coarsely chopped
1 tomato, diced
$^1/_3$ cup bottled Italian or vinaigrette salad dressing
1 tablespoon minced fresh cilantro
1 tablespoon minced fresh chives
$^1/_4$ cup (1 oz.) crumbled feta cheese

1. Place pork in large resealable bag. In small bowl, combine lime juice, water, cilantro, jalapeño, salt, garlic, cumin and pepper; mix well. Pour mixture over meat. Seal bag; refrigerate 2 hours, turning occasionally.

2. In large bowl, combine bell peppers, cucumber, onion, jicama and tomato; mix well. Add salad dressing, cilantro, chives and feta cheese; toss well. Season with salt and pepper.

3. Heat grill. Remove pork from bag; discard marinade. Place pork on gas grill over medium heat or on charcoal grill 4 to 6 inches from medium coals. Cook about 8 minutes per side. Season with salt and pepper, if desired.

4. Divide gazpacho evenly on four large plates. Top with pork tenderloin pieces. Garnish with olives and herbs.

4 servings.

THAILAND CHICKEN

Carrie Robinson

1 tablespoon kosher (coarse) salt
1 (12-oz.) pkg. fettuccine
2 cups chunky picante sauce
$1/2$ cup chunky peanut butter
$1/4$ cup honey
$1/4$ cup fresh orange juice
2 teaspoons low-sodium soy sauce
1 teaspoon grated fresh ginger
2 tablespoons vegetable oil
6 ($1^1/2$ lb.) boneless skinless chicken
   breast halves
$1/8$ teaspoon salt
$1/8$ teaspoon freshly ground pepper
$1^1/2$ tablespoons chopped fresh
   cilantro or parsley

1. Heat grill.

2. Fill large pot two-thirds full of water; add 1 tablespoon salt. Bring to a boil over high heat. Cook fettuccine according to package directions; drain.

3. Meanwhile, in small saucepan, combine picante sauce, peanut butter, honey, orange juice, soy sauce and ginger. Cook over low heat, stirring constantly, until blended. Reserve $1/4$ cup of the mixture; toss remaining mixture with fettuccine and place on serving platter. Keep warm.

4. Coat chicken with oil; season with salt and pepper. Place chicken on gas grill over medium heat or on charcoal grill 4 to 6 inches from medium coals. Cook chicken 5 to 7 minutes per side or until internal temperature reaches at least 160°F.

5. Arrange chicken over fettuccine; spoon reserved sauce over chicken. Garnish with cilantro or parsley.

4 to 6 servings.

CHIPOTLE-HONEY GLAZED PORK WITH CHIMCHURRI SAUCE

*Julie Dematteo
Clementon, New Jersey*

MARINADE
2 ($3/4$-lb.) pork tenderloins, trimmed
6 tablespoons honey
2 tablespoons Dijon mustard
2 canned chipotle peppers in adobo
   sauce, finely minced
3 tablespoons plus 4 teaspoons fresh
   lemon juice

CHIMCHURRI SAUCE
$1^1/2$ cups chopped fresh Italian parsley
$1/2$ cup olive oil
3 garlic cloves, minced

1. Place pork in large resealable plastic bag. In medium bowl, combine honey, mustard, chipotle pepper and 4 teaspoons of the lemon juice; mix well. Pour mixture over pork. Seal bag; refrigerate 2 hours.

2. Meanwhile, combine parsley, oil, garlic and remaining 3 tablespoons lemon juice in small bowl. Set aside at room temperature.

3. Heat grill. Remove pork from marinade; discard marinade. Place pork on gas grill over medium heat or on charcoal grill 4 to 6 inches from medium coals. Cook about 25 minutes or until slightly pink in center, turning occasionally. Let stand 5 minutes, then thinly slice. Serve with sauce.

4 servings.

CALYPSO CHICKEN WITH BANANA SALSA

Shirley Desantis
Bethlehem, Pennsylvania

MARINADE
1/4 cup fresh lime juice
2 tablespoons extra-virgin olive oil
1 garlic clove, minced
12 boneless skinless chicken breast
   thighs, cut into 1-inch pieces

BANANA CHIPOTLE SALSA
4 ripe bananas, peeled, halved
   lengthwise, sliced (1/4-inch thick)
1 red bell pepper, chopped
1/3 cup chopped fresh cilantro
1/2 cup chopped pistachios
2 teaspoons minced chipotle chiles in
   adobo sauce
2 tablespoons extra-virgin olive oil
2 tablespoons honey
1 tablespoon fresh lime juice
1/8 teaspoon salt

1. Place chicken in large resealable plastic bag. In small bowl, combine 1/4 cup lime juice, 2 tablespoons oil and garlic; mix well. Pour marinade over chicken. Seal bag; refrigerate 4 hours.

2. In large bowl combine bananas, bell pepper, cilantro, pistachios and chipotles; mix well. In another small bowl, whisk together 2 tablespoons oil, honey and 1 tablespoon lime juice; add to banana mixture and stir gently. Season with salt.

3. Heat grill. Remove chicken from marinade; discard marinade. Thread chicken on 6 (10- to 12-inch) metal skewers. Place skewers on gas grill over medium heat or on charcoal grill 4 to 6 inches from medium coals. Cook, about 10 minutes, or until browned and no longer pink in center, turning as needed. Serve chicken with salsa.

6 servings.

MOLASSES-RUM PORK CHOPS WITH GRILLED PINEAPPLE

Karen Patn
Auburn Hills, Michigan

SAUCE
2 tablespoons olive oil
1 medium onion, minced
2 tablespoons minced fresh ginger
2 tablespoons minced garlic
1 cup dark rum
1/2 cup red wine vinegar
1 cup ketchup
1/2 cup molasses
1/4 cup packed brown sugar
1 tablespoon ground allspice

MEAT
9 (8-oz.) boneless pork chops (1 inch
   thick)
2 tablespoons olive oil
1/8 teaspoon salt
1/8 teaspoon freshly ground pepper
2 (8-oz.) cans pineapple rings, drained

1. Heat grill.

2. In large saucepan, heat oil on gas grill over medium heat or on charcoal grill 4 to 6 inches from medium coals. Add onions to saucepan; sauté 5 minutes. Add ginger and garlic; sauté an additional 5 minutes. Add rum, vinegar, ketchup, molasses, brown sugar and allspice. Bring to a boil; remove from grill.

3. Rub pork chops with olive oil, salt and pepper. Cook 10 to 12 minutes per side or until no longer pink in center.

4. Just before pork chops are done, place pineapple rings on grill. Cook 3 to 4 minutes per side. Brush chops and pineapple with sauce.

8 servings.

GRILLED WRAPPED SHRIMP

Joyce Serrano
Twentynine Palms, California

1 lb. shelled, deveined uncooked
   jumbo shrimp*
$1/2$ lb. thick-sliced bacon, halved
   (about 10 slices)
1 cup honey-smoked barbecue sauce

1. Heat grill.

2. Wrap each shrimp with one-half strip of bacon; secure with toothpick.

3. Place shrimp on top rack of gas grill over medium heat or on charcoal grill 4 to 6 inches from medium coals. Cook 2 minutes per side. Brush shrimp with sauce; cook 8 to 10 minutes or until bacon is crisp and shrimp turns pink. Heat remainder of sauce to a boil for dipping.

4 servings.

TIP *For a spicier taste, place one thin slice pepper-Jack cheese between bacon and shrimp prior to grilling.

GREMOLATA SALMON BURGERS WITH TAPENADE MAYO

Julie Dematteo
Clementon, New Jersey

TAPENADE MAYO
5 large pitted kalamata olives, minced
$1^1/2$ tablespoons olive oil
4 large fresh basil leaves, minced
1 tablespoon chopped fresh parsley
1 teaspoon Dijon mustard
$1/2$ teaspoon capers, rinsed, chopped
1 garlic clove, minced
6 tablespoons mayonnaise

BURGERS
$1^1/4$ lb. skinned salmon fillets, finely ground
$3/4$ cup fresh bread crumbs
1 egg, beaten
6 green onions, finely chopped
$1/2$ cup chopped fresh parsley
4 garlic cloves, minced
2 tablespoons Dijon mustard
1 tablespoon grated lemon peel
$1/2$ teaspoon each salt, freshly ground pepper
2 teaspoons fresh thyme
6 large sandwich rolls, split
1 bunch watercress, stems removed

1. Heat grill. In medium bowl, combine olives, olive oil, basil, parsley, mustard, capers, garlic and mayonnaise; mix well. Refrigerate, covered, until ready to use. In large bowl, combine ground salmon, bread crumbs, egg, onion, parsley, garlic, mustard, lemon peel, salt, pepper and thyme; mix well. Shape mixture into 6 (1-inch-thick) patties.

2. Place patties on gas grill over medium heat or charcoal grill over medium coals 4 to 6 inches from medium coals. Cook 4 to 6 minutes per side or until cooked through, turning once. During last few minutes of cooking time, toast rolls. Spread mayonnaise mixture on cut sides of rolls. Place burgers on bottom halves and top with generous amount of watercress. Replace roll tops.

6 servings.

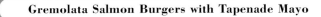

Gremolata Salmon Burgers with Tapenade Mayo

FIESTA FLANK STEAK WITH CARAMELIZED ONION

David Rothschild
Phoenix, Arizona

MARINADE
1 (12-oz.) can stout beer
$1/2$ cup dark corn syrup
2 tablespoons vegetable oil
$1/2$ cup fresh lime juice
1 teaspoon dried oregano
$1/2$ teaspoon garlic chile paste
3 garlic cloves, finely minced
$1/8$ teaspoon salt
$1/8$ teaspoon freshly ground pepper

MEAT
1 ($1^1/2$ lb.) flank or skirt steak
2 large onions, thinly sliced
1 (16-oz.) pkg. flour tortillas

1. In large bowl, combine beer, corn syrup, oil, lime juice, oregano, chile paste, garlic, salt and pepper; mix well. Place steak and onions in large resealable plastic bag; pour marinade over steak. Seal bag; refrigerate 1 hour.

2. Heat grill. Remove steak from marinade, keeping onions in marinade. Place steak on gas grill over medium heat or on charcoal grill 4 to 6 inches from medium coals. Cook 5 to 7 minutes per side or until no longer pink in center.

3. Meanwhile, pour onions and marinade into large skillet; cook on grill until all liquid evaporates and onions are glazed with marinade.

4. Remove meat to cutting board; let rest 10 minutes. Warm tortillas on turned-off grill; wrap in foil to keep warm.

5. Slice steak as thinly as possible against grain of meat. Mound onions onto serving platter and fan steak out over bed of onions. Garnish with chopped cilantro. Serve with tortillas, rice or beans, salsa, guacamole and sour cream.

4 servings.

TACO INSIDE-OUTS

Beverly Coyode
Gasport, New York

1 cup (4 oz.) shredded cheddar
  cheese
$1/2$ cup crushed corn chips
$1/4$ cup taco or barbecue sauce
1 lb. hot dogs

1. Heat grill.

2. In small bowl, combine cheese, chips and taco sauce. Cut narrow slit in each hot dog to create picket. Insert about 2 tablespoons cheese mixture into each hot dog. Place on 4 (10- to 12-inch) metal skewers.

3. Place skewers on gas grill over medium heat or on charcoal grill 4 to 6 inches from medium coals. Cook hot dogs 3 to 5 minutes or until heated and cheese melts.

4 to 6 servings.

FLANK STEAK MARINADE

Tiffany Fletcher
Leavenworth, Washington

1 (1-lb.) flank steak
$1/2$ cup low-sodium soy sauce
$1/2$ cup water
$1/2$ cup fresh apple, orange or
  pineapple juice
$1/2$ cup packed brown sugar
$1/8$ teaspoon garlic powder

1. Place steak in large resealable plastic bag. In small bowl, whisk together soy sauce, water, juice, brown sugar and garlic powder; mix well. Pour marinade over steak. Seal bag; refrigerate 4 hours, turning once every hour.

2. Heat grill. Remove steak from marinade; discard marinade. Place steak on gas grill over medium heat or on charcoal grill 4 to 6 inches from medium coals. Cook until internal temperature reaches 160°F.

4 to 6 servings.

BBQ SOUTHWESTERN CHICKEN PIZZA

Kari Cashmore
Ingleside, Illinois

2 (1-lb.) boneless skinless chicken
   breast halves, cut into 1-inch pieces
2 tablespoons olive oil
1 teaspoon paprika
1 teaspoon ground cumin
1 teaspoon chili powder
3 garlic cloves, minced
1/4 teaspoon crushed red pepper
1 tablespoon fresh lime juice
1 medium red onion
2 tablespoons butter
1 tablespoon packed brown sugar
1 (12-inch) prebaked Italian pizza
   crust
1 cup barbecue sauce
1 cup (4 oz.) shredded Monterey Jack
   cheese
1/2 cup (2 oz.) shredded mozzarella
   cheese
1/2 cup (2 oz.) shredded cheddar
   cheese

1. Place chicken in large resealable plastic bag. In medium bowl, whisk together oil, paprika, cumin, chili powder, garlic, red pepper and lime juice. Pour over chicken to coat. Seal bag; refrigerate up to 24 hours.

2. Heat grill. Remove chicken from marinade; discard marinade. In large skillet, brown chicken over medium heat about 5 minutes or until chicken is no longer pink in center. Set aside. In same skillet, sauté onion with butter and brown sugar over medium-low heat until onion is tender and caramelized.

3. Brush barbecue sauce over pizza crust. Spread cooked chicken evenly over sauce. Top with cooked onion and cheese.

4. Place pizza on gas grill over medium heat or on charcoal grill 4 to 6 inches from medium coals. Cook until cheese is bubbly and melted.

6 servings.

WEST TEXAS DESERT BURGERS

Sharon & Gene Smith
Midland, Texas

1 1/2 lb. ground beef or sirloin
1 (4- or 7-oz.) can chopped green
   chiles, drained
1/8 teaspoon salt
1/8 teaspoon freshly ground pepper
2 tablespoons oil
1 cup chopped white onion
4 onion rolls, sliced, buttered
4 (1-oz.) slices pepper-Jack cheese

1. In large bowl, combine beef, chiles, salt and pepper; mix well. Form mixture into 4 (1-inch-thick) patties. Refrigerate 1 hour.

2. In large skillet, heat oil over medium-high heat until hot. Sauté onions until light brown and crisp.

3. Heat grill. Place patties on gas grill over medium heat or on charcoal grill 4 to 6 inches from medium coals. Cook patties until no longer pink in center. Lightly toast rolls on grill. Top patties with 1 slice cheese and sautéed onions. Garnish with mayonnaise, lettuce, tomato and jalapeño chile. Serve with potato wedges and grilled vegetables, if desired.

4 servings.

Grilled Sea Bass with Tomatillo Salsa

GRILLED SEA BASS WITH TOMATILLO SALSA

David King
St. Paul, Minnesota

20 medium tomatillos, peeled
1 1/2 tablespoons olive oil
3/4 cup finely minced red onions
3 jalapeño chiles, seeded, minced
1 tablespoon freshly ground pepper
1 1/2 tablespoons minced garlic
3 tablespoons honey
2 cups reduced-sodium vegetable broth
1 lime, halved
1 tablespoon kosher (coarse) salt
4 (8-oz.) sea bass fillets
1/4 cup chopped fresh cilantro

1. Heat broiler. Arrange tomatillos on baking sheet. Broil 4 to 6 inches from heat 6 to 8 minutes or until blackened on 1 side. Remove to food processor or blender, including all juices; blend until smooth.

2. In large skillet, heat oil over medium-high heat until hot. Sauté onions, jalapeños and pepper about 10 minutes or until onion starts to brown. Add garlic; sauté until fragrant. Add tomatillo mixture, honey, stock and juice from half of the lime. Simmer 10 minutes; season with salt. Simmer an additional 10 minutes; remove from heat. (Sauce can be prepared up to two days ahead. Cover and refrigerate)

3. Heat grill. Lightly brush sea bass with olive oil; season with salt and pepper. Place fish on gas grill over medium heat or on charcoal grill 4 to 6 inches from medium coals. Cook, turning once, 14 to 16 minutes or until fish flakes easily with fork. Use fork to remove.

4. Pour tomatillo sauce over fish; sprinkle with chopped fresh cilantro. Garnish with lime.

4 to 6 servings.

INDIAN GARBANZO BURGERS

Ellen Berg
Portland, Oregon

3 (15-oz.) cans garbanzo beans, rinsed, drained
5 tomatoes, peeled, seeded, diced
6 green onions, finely chopped
1/2 cup chopped fresh cilantro
3 tablespoons freshly grated ginger
2 teaspoons ground cumin
1 tablespoon garam masala*
1/4 teaspoon cayenne pepper
1/8 teaspoon salt
2 eggs, beaten
1/4 cup olive oil
3 cups dry bread crumbs

1. In food processor or blender, combine beans with half of the diced tomatoes; blend, adding water as needed to make smooth mixture.

2. Transfer mixture to large bowl; add remaining tomatoes, green onions, cilantro, ginger, cumin, garam masala, cayenne pepper, salt, eggs, oil and bread crumbs. Mix thoroughly with large spoon or hands until mixture holds patty shape well. Add water if mixture is too dry. Form 16 (4-inch) patties.

3. Heat grill. Place patties on gas grill over medium heat or on charcoal grill 4 to 6 inches from medium coals. Cook 5 to 8 minutes per side or until lightly browned. Serve hot with lime wedges and yogurt, if desired.

8 servings.

TIP *Garam masala is a blend of spices from India that varies from region to region. You can purchase it in the specialty section of most larger grocery stores.

SNAPPY APPLE TURKEY BURGERS

*Shirley Desantis
Bethlehem, Pennsylvania*

BURGERS
1/4 cup apple butter
1 tablespoon horseradish
1 tablespoon Dijon mustard
1 1/2 lb. lean ground turkey breast
1/4 cup dry bread crumbs
1/8 teaspoon salt
1/8 teaspoon freshly ground pepper

GLAZE
1/2 cup apple butter
2 tablespoons ketchup
1 tablespoon balsamic vinegar

GARNISHES
2 to 3 medium apples, sliced
1 medium red onion, sliced
6 hamburger rolls
6 large lettuce leaves

1. Heat grill. In medium bowl, combine 1/4 cup apple butter, horseradish and mustard; mix well. Add turkey and bread crumbs; mix gently but thoroughly until just combined. Divide into 6 (1-inch-thick) patties. Refrigerate until ready to grill. In small bowl, stir together 1/2 cup apple butter, ketchup and balsamic vinegar; reserve 1/3 of the glaze.

2. Place patties on gas grill over medium heat or on charcoal grill 4 to 6 inches from medium coals. Lightly brush patties with glaze; season with salt and pepper. Turn over; brush other side lightly with glaze. Season with salt and pepper. Cook patties 6 minutes per side or until no longer pink in center..

3. Meanwhile, place apple and onion slices on grill; brush lightly with glaze. Grill about 4 minutes per side or until browned and tender, turning once. During last few minutes of grill time, lightly toast buns. To serve, place lettuce leaf on bottom of each bun; top with onion slice and patty. Brush with glaze, then top with apple slice and top of bun.

6 servings.

PEPPERED RIB EYE STEAKS

*Tammy Raynes
Natchitoches, Louisiana*

4 beef rib-eye steaks (1 1/2 inches thick)
1 tablespoon vegetable oil
1 tablespoon garlic powder
1 tablespoon paprika
2 teaspoons dried thyme
2 teaspoons dried oregano
1 1/2 teaspoons freshly ground pepper
1 teaspoon salt
1 teaspoon lemon pepper
1 teaspoon cayenne pepper

1. Place steaks in large resealable plastic bag. In small bowl, combine oil, garlic powder, paprika, thyme, oregano, pepper, salt, lemon pepper and cayenne; mix well. Pour mixture over steaks. Seal bag; refrigerate at least 1 hour.

2. Heat grill. Remove steaks from marinade; discard marinade. Place steaks on gas grill over medium heat or on charcoal grill 4 to 6 inches from medium coals. Cook until meat is cooked to desired doneness, turning once. Cut across grain into thick slices.

8 servings.

GRILLED CHICKEN SALAD WITH STRAWBERRY VINAIGRETTE DRESSING

Chris Uecker
Big Bend, Wisconsin

DRESSING
1¹/₂ cups ripe strawberries
¹/₄ cup honey
¹/₄ cup balsamic vinegar
³/₄ cups olive oil
Dash salt

SALAD
6 (1-lb.) boneless skinless chicken
  breast halves
8 cups mixed salad greens
3 cups sliced strawberries
3 avocados, sliced
2 cups pitted halved cherry tomatoes
1 cucumber, sliced
3 cups farfalle (bow-tie pasta), cooled

1. In food processor or blender, puree strawberries, honey and vinegar. Slowly drizzle in oil. Season with salt.

2. Place chicken in resealable plastic bag; pour ³/₄ cup of the dressing over chicken. Seal bag; refrigerate at least 30 minutes, turning once.

3. Divide salad greens evenly among 4 plates. Top with equal amounts strawberries, avocado and pasta. Arrange tomatoes and cucumbers around outside of plate.

4. Heat grill. Remove chicken from bag; discard marinade. Place chicken on gas grill over medium heat or on charcoal grill 4 to 6 inches from medium coals. Cook 5 minutes; turn and baste with strawberry dressing to coat. Grill an additional 5 to 8 minutes or until no longer pink in center. Remove chicken from grill.

5. Arrange 1 chicken breast per plate in middle of salad. Top with croutons and drizzle with remaining strawberry dressing. Serve immediately with garlic cheese bread, if desired.

4 servings.

TEXAS PASTRAMI

Debby Pfeiffer
Canyon Lake, Texas

2 tablespoons black peppercorns
3 tablespoons dried thyme
6 whole bay leaves, crumbled
4 large garlic cloves
2 teaspoons cumin seed
6 cups water
³/₄ cup pure maple syrup
³/₄ cup kosher (coarse) salt
1 (4-lb.) beef brisket
²/₃ cup freshly ground pepper
1 tablespoon crushed red pepper
16 dried chile pasilla

1. In small bowl combine peppercorns, thyme, bay leaves, cloves, garlic and cumin; mix well.

2. In large saucepan bring water, syrup and salt to a boil over medium heat. Stir to dissolve. Remove saucepan from heat; add peppercorn mixture. Steep.

3. Place brisket in large resealable plastic bag; pour marinade over brisket. Seal bag; refrigerate 3 weeks, turning brisket every couple of days.

4. Heat grill. In medium bowl, combine black pepper, red pepper and chile pasilla. Press mixture into meat. Wrap brisket in foil. Place on gas grill over medium heat or charcoal grill 4 to 6 inches from medium coals until internal temperature reaches 170°F.

4 servings.

STUFFED PORK CHOPS

Sandy Riley
Sheridan, Wyoming

8 center-cut loin pork chops
   (1 inch thick)
1 cup dry bread crumbs
$1/2$ cup finely chopped cashews
2 teaspoons minced onion
2 tablespoons chopped fresh parsley
$1/2$ teaspoon crushed red pepper
$1/4$ cup margarine, melted
1 tablespoon water
$3/4$ teaspoon salt
$1/4$ cup Dijon mustard
2 tablespoons olive oil
2 tablespoons honey

1. Heat grill.

2. Cut pocket on bone side of each pork chop to hold stuffing. In medium bowl, combine bread crumbs, cashews, onion, parsley and crushed pepper; mix well. In small bowl, combine margarine, water and salt; mix well. Pour margarine mixture over crumb mixture; toss. Stuff chops with mixture.

3. In small pan, combine mustard, oil and honey; warm over medium heat.

4. Place pork on gas grill over medium-high heat or on charcoal grill 4 to 6 inches from medium coals. Cover and cook 35 to 40 minutes or until internal temperature reaches 170°F. During last 20 minutes of cooking, turn pork 3 or 4 times and brush with mustard mixture 2 or 3 times.

8 servings.

TUSCAN PORK TENDERLOIN WITH FENNEL AND CANNELLINI BEANS

Shirley Desantis
Bethlehem, Pennsylvania

2 (1-lb.) pork tenderloins
$1/8$ teaspoon salt
$1/8$ teaspoon freshly ground pepper
4 fennel bulbs, rinsed, fronds
   removed (reserve some fronds for
   garnish), quartered, sliced
   ($1/3$ inch thick)
$1/4$ cup plus 2 tablespoons Italian
   roasted garlic salad dressing
2 (16-oz.) cans cannellini beans,
   rinsed, drained
4 green onions, thinly sliced
$1/4$ cup coarsely chopped roasted red
   bell pepper
2 teaspoons minced fresh rosemary

1. Heat grill. Trim excess fat from pork. If loin has a thin narrow point, turn under and secure with toothpick. Season lightly with salt and pepper. Season fennel slices with salt and pepper.

2. In aluminum foil, mix 2 tablespoons of the salad dressing, beans, green onions, red pepper and rosemary; season with salt and black pepper. Close packet and fold tightly.

3. Place pork on gas grill over medium heat or on charcoal grill 4 to 6 inches from medium coals; brush lightly with salad dressing. Cook about 20 minutes, turning once and brushing with dressing, or until internal temperature reaches at least 160°F. Place foil on grill. Cook 10 minutes, turning once. Place fennel slices on grill; brush with dressing. Grill 5 to 6 minutes per side, brush with dressing when turning. Fennel should be crisp-tender.

4. Remove all food to cutting board. Let pork rest 5 minutes, lightly covered, before slicing. Arrange bean mixture in center of large platter, and place pork and fennel slices alternately around beans. Garnish with reserved fronds.

6 servings.

Tuscan Pork Tenderloin with Fennel and Cannellini Beans

BLACKENED SHRIMP SALAD WITH SPICED BANANAS & TROPICAL VINAIGRETTE

Julie Dematteo
Clementon, New Jersey

VINAIGRETTE
$1/4$ cup each pineapple and orange-
   banana juice blend
1 tablespoon fresh lime juice
2 teaspoons honey
$1^1/2$ teaspoons Dijon mustard
$1/8$ teaspoon salt
1 chipotle chile in adobo sauce,
   minced
3 tablespoons olive oil

SPICED BANANAS
$1/2$ teaspoon grated lime peel
$1/2$ teaspoon cinnamon
$1/2$ teaspoon ground allspice
$1/4$ teaspoon salt
4 teaspoons fresh lime juice
2 medium firm ripe bananas, sliced
   ($1/4$ inch thick)

SALAD
1 lb. shelled, deveined uncooked
   jumbo shrimp
2 tablespoons olive oil
2 tablespoons Cajun seasoning
8 cups mixed salad greens

1. Heat grill. Lightly brush rack with oil. In medium bowl, whisk together juice blend, lime juice, honey, mustard, salt, chipotle chile and olive oil. In another medium bowl, whisk together lime peel, cinnamon, allspice, salt, lime juice and bananas. Brush shrimp with olive oil; toss with Cajun seasoning.

2. Place shrimp on gas grill over medium heat or on charcoal grill 4 to 6 inches from medium coals. Cook 6 to 8 minutes or until shrimp turn pink.

3. Toss greens with enough dressing to coat; divide evenly among 4 large salad plates. Top with shrimp; pour banana mixture over greens.

4 servings.

MAGICAL PICNIC BURGERS

Kathy Hickey
Ashley, Pennsylvania

$1^1/2$ lb. ground beef, turkey, lamb or
   pork
2 tablespoons chopped onion
1 teaspoon salt
Dash freshly ground pepper
6 to 12 thick slices bacon
6 hot dog buns, toasted, halved

1. Heat grill.

2. In large bowl, combine meat, onion, salt and pepper; mix well. Shape mixture into 6 (1-inch-thick) patties. Spiral bacon strips around; secure with wooden toothpicks.

3. Place patties on gas grill over medium heat or on charcoal grill 4 to 6 inches from medium coals 5 to 10 minutes or until patties are no longer pink in center and bacon is crisp. During last 2 minutes of cooking, lightly toast hot dog buns. Place patty on bun; remove toothpick.

6 servings.

CIDER-MARINATED STUFFED PORK TENDERLOIN

Tim Husband
Jackson, Wyoming

1 cup apple cider
4 tablespoons Dijon mustard
2 tablespoons minced fresh rosemary
6 garlic cloves, minced
2 teaspoons freshly ground pepper
2 tablespoons olive oil
6 (8-oz.) pork tenderloins
$^1/_2$ lb. bacon
1 shallot, diced
1 lb. spinach, stems removed
2 tablespoons balsamic vinegar
2 cups dry bread crumbs
$^1/_8$ teaspoon each salt, freshly ground
   pepper

1. In small bowl, combine cider, 3 tablespoons of the mustard, rosemary, 4 garlic cloves , pepper and oil; mix well.

2. Place pork in 3-quart casserole. Pour marinade over pork; cover and refrigerate at least 3 hours. In large skillet, cook bacon over medium-high heat until crisp. Remove bacon from skillet; drain on paper towels. Pour off all but 2 tablespoons of the bacon fat. Add shallot and remaining 2 garlic cloves; sauté over medium heat until shallots are transparent. Increase heat to medium-high; cook spinach until wilted. Transfer spinach to colander; drain. Remove spinach to large bowl. Add bacon, vinegar, remaining 1 tablespoon mustard and bread crumbs; toss gently.

3. Remove pork from marinade; discard marinade. Drain pork. Insert sharp, thin bladed knife through center of each tenderloin lengthwise. Gently create pocket using fingers; stuff each tenderloin with spinach mixture. (Tenderloin may be prepared to this point up to four hours in advance.

4. Heat grill. Season pork with salt and pepper. Place pork on gas grill over medium heat or on charcoal grill 4 to 6 inches from medium coals. Cook 25 minutes, turning occasionally.

8 to 10 servings.

MARINATED BEEF KABOBS

Jennifer Okutman
Westminster, Maryland

1 (1-lb.) sirloin steak, cut into 1-inch
   pieces
1$^1/_2$ cups olive oil
$^3/_4$ cup low-sodium soy sauce
$^1/_4$ cup Worcestershire sauce
2 tablespoons dry mustard
2$^1/_4$ teaspoons salt
1 tablespoon freshly ground pepper
$^1/_2$ cup wine vinegar
1$^1/_2$ cups chopped fresh parsley
2 garlic cloves, crushed
$^1/_3$ cup fresh lemon juice
Assorted 1-inch vegetable pieces
   (cherry tomatoes, zucchini,
   mushrooms, etc.)

1. Place steak in large resealable plastic bag. In large bowl, combine olive oil, soy sauce, Worcestershire sauce, mustard, salt, pepper, wine vinegar, parsley, garlic and lemon juice; mix well. Pour marinade over steak. Seal bag; refrigerate 4 hours.

2. Heat grill. Remove steak from marinade; discard marinade. Alternately, thread steak and vegetables on 4 (8- to 10-inch) metal skewers. Place skewers on gas grill over medium heat or on charcoal grill 4 to 6 inches from medium coals. Cook to desired doneness.

4 servings.

NORTHWOOD'S CHICKEN BURGERS WITH MAPLE MUSTARD GLAZE

Jamie Miller
Maple Grove, Minnesota

2 cups apple or hickory wood chips
$1^1/_4$ lb. ground chicken or turkey
1 tablespoon minced fresh thyme
1 tablespoon minced fresh sage
$1^1/_2$ tablespoons Worcestershire sauce
1 teaspoon liquid smoke
1 teaspoon kosher (coarse) salt
$^1/_2$ teaspoon freshly ground pepper
$^1/_2$ cup pure maple syrup
$^1/_2$ cup Dijon mustard
1 tablespoon balsamic vinegar
$^1/_2$ teaspoon cayenne pepper
4 thick slices sweet onion
4 (1-oz.) slices Gruyère or Swiss cheese
4 large kaiser rolls

1. Soak wood chips in water 30 minutes. Heat grill. In large bowl, combine chicken, thyme, sage, Worcestershire sauce, liquid smoke, salt and pepper; mix well. Shape mixture into 4 (1-inch-thick) patties.

2. In small saucepan, whisk together syrup, mustard, vinegar and cayenne pepper. Place saucepan of glaze on edge of grill; whisk occasionally. Drain wood chips and place in aluminum foil packet, leaving top of packet open. Place packet on top of coals.

3. Place patties on gas grill over medium heat or on charcoal grill 4 to 6 inches from medium coals. Cook about 7 minutes on first side. Meanwhile, brush onion slices with glaze and grill with patties. Turn patties, brush with glaze and top with cheese. Turn onions, brush with glaze and cover grill, vents open. Grill an additional 5 to 7 minutes or until patties are no longer pink in center and onions are golden. After removing patties and onions from grill, lightly toast buns, cut side down.

4. Brush bottom of bun with glaze, top with chicken patty, drizzle with 1 tablespoon glaze and top with onion slice. Brush top of bun with glaze and place on top of onion.

4 servings.

SOUTHWESTERN CHICKEN SALAD

Kathy Woodman
Wichita, Kansas

3 tablespoons olive oil
1 tablespoon red wine vinegar
$^3/_4$ teaspoon salt
$^1/_4$ teaspoon freshly ground pepper
$^1/_4$ teaspoon chili powder
$^1/_2$ teaspoon ground cumin
3 boneless skinless chicken breast halves
1 large ripe tomato, cut into large chunks
1 (8-oz.) bag field greens
1 cup corn kernels
$^1/_2$ cup chopped cilantro

1. Heat grill.

2. In small bowl, whisk together oil, vinegar, $^1/_4$ teaspoon of the salt and pepper until thoroughly blended; set aside.

3. In another small bowl, mix chili powder, cumin and remaining $^1/_2$ teaspoon salt. Sprinkle over chicken.

4. Place chicken on gas grill over medium heat or on charcoal grill 4 to 6 inches from medium coals. Cook about 10 minutes, turning once, or until internal temperature reaches at least 160°F.

5. Remove chicken to clean cutting board; cut into 1-inch pieces. Place chicken in large serving bowl with tomatoes, greens, corn and cilantro. pour dressing over; toss to mix and thoroughly coat.

4 servings.

POULTRY PLUS

CHICKEN CACCIATORE

Tom Dello Stritto
Auburn, New York

$^1/_2$ cup all-purpose flour
$1^1/_4$ teaspoons freshly ground pepper
1 teaspoon salt
1 ($3^1/_2$-lb.) broiler-fryer chicken, cut
  into serving pieces
$^1/_4$ cup olive oil
3 thick slices bacon, chopped
1 small green bell pepper, chopped
1 cup tomato sauce
1 (8-oz.) pkg. mushrooms, sliced
$^1/_2$ cup dry red wine
2 garlic cloves, minced
1 medium onion, chopped
1 teaspoon dried oregano
$^1/_4$ cup sliced ripe olives
1 bay leaf
1 (28-oz.) can Italian tomatoes,
  drained, chopped

1. In large resealable plastic bag, combine flour, $^1/_4$ teaspoon of the pepper and salt. Rinse chicken and pat dry. Add chicken to bag; shake to coat.

2. In Dutch oven, heat oil over medium-high heat until hot. Cook chicken and bacon until browned on all sides. Drain oil. Stir in bell peppers, tomato sauce, mushrooms, wine, garlic, onions, oregano, remaining 1 teaspoon pepper, olives and bay leaf. Break up tomatoes with fork; add to chicken mixture.

3. Heat until boiling; cover and reduce heat to a simmer. Cook about 45 minutes or until chicken is no longer pink in center. Discard bay leaf.

6 servings.

LEMON-HERB ROAST CHICKEN

David A. Heppner
Brandon, Florida

$^1/_2$ cup butter, softened
2 tablespoons chopped fresh rosemary
  or 2 teaspoons dried
2 tablespoons chopped fresh thyme or
  2 teaspoons dried
3 large garlic cloves, minced
$1^1/_4$ teaspoons grated lemon peel
$^1/_8$ teaspoon each salt, freshly ground
  pepper
1 ($6^1/_2$ - to 7-lb.) roasting chicken
$^1/_4$ cup dry white wine
1 cup reduced-sodium chicken broth
2 tablespoons all-purpose flour

1. Heat oven to 450°F.

2. In small bowl, combine butter, rosemary, thyme, garlic and lemon peel; stir to blend. Add salt and pepper.

3. Rinse chicken and pat dry. Slide hand under skin of chicken to loosen skin from meat. Reserve 2 tablespoons herb butter for gravy. Rub half of remaining butter over chicken breast under skin. Spread remaining butter over outside of chicken. Season chicken with remaining salt and pepper.

4. Place chicken in large heavy roasting pan. Bake 20 minutes; reduce oven temperature to 375°F. Bake $1^1/_4$ hours. Lift chicken and tilt slightly, removing excess juices from cavity into roasting pan. Transfer chicken to platter; tent with aluminum foil to keep warm. Pour pan juices into large glass measuring cup. Spoon fat off top.

5. Pour wine into roasting pan; boil wine over high heat, scraping up any browned bits. Stir wine into measuring cup. Add enough broth to measure $2^1/_4$ cups liquid. In small skillet, melt reserved 2 tablespoons herb butter over medium-high heat. Add flour; whisk about 3 minutes or until smooth. Gradually whisk in pan juices. Boil 7 minutes or until thickened to sauce consistency, whisking occasionally.

4 to 6 servings.

Lemon-Herb Roast Chicken

SUNDAY CHICKEN SUPPER

Tammy Raynes
Natchitoches, New Mexico

1 (3$^{1}/_2$- to 4-lb.) broiler-fryer chicken, cut up
4 carrots, cut into 2-inch pieces
1 onion, chopped
1 rib celery, cut into 2-inch pieces
2 cups fresh green beans, cut into 2-inch pieces
5 red potatoes, quartered
4 thick slices bacon, cooked, crumbled
1$^{1}/_2$ cups hot water
2 teaspoons chicken bouillon granules
1 teaspoon salt
$^{1}/_2$ teaspoon dried thyme
$^{1}/_2$ teaspoon dried basil
$^{1}/_8$ teaspoon freshly ground pepper

1. Rinse chicken and pat dry. In slow cooker, layer carrots, onion, celery, green beans, potatoes, chicken and bacon.

2. In small bowl, combine water, bouillon, salt, thyme, basil and pepper; mix well. Pour over bacon but do not stir.

3. Cover and cook on low heat setting 6 to 8 hours or until vegetables are tender and chicken juices run clear. Remove chicken and vegetables. Thicken juices for gravy, if desired.

4 servings.

CHICKEN LEGS MEDITERRANEAN

Terrance Smith
Merritt Island, Florida

8 chicken drumsticks
8 (3- x 3-inch) slices mozzarella cheese
$^{1}/_2$ cup virgin olive oil
$^{1}/_4$ cup herbes de Provence
4 garlic cloves, thinly sliced
2 large eggs, beaten
$^{1}/_8$ teaspoon salt
$^{1}/_8$ teaspoon freshly ground pepper
$^{1}/_2$ cup all-purpose flour
4 oz. macadamia nuts, finely chopped

1. Heat oven to 350°F. Spray 13x9-inch pan with nonstick cooking spray.

2. Rinse drumsticks and pat dry. Using sharp, thin-bladed knife, cut close to and all around bone about $^{3}/_4$ of the way down, creating pocket.

3. Moisten one side of cheese slice lightly with oil. Sprinkle with 1 teaspoon herbes de Provence; place $^{1}/_2$ sliced garlic clove on cheese. Fit cheese into pocket, seasoned side toward bone; push up meat to hide cheese. Repeat with each drumstick.

4. In small bowl, whisk remaining of herbes de Provence into egg. Season with salt and pepper. Coat each drumstick with flour, then dip into egg mixture. Roll each drumstick in nuts.

5. In large skillet, heat remaining oil over medium-high heat until hot. Cook drumsticks, about 8 to 10 minutes or until brown on all sides. Remove from skillet. Arrange drumsticks on pan; bake 20 minutes or until juices run clear.

6. Cover serving plate with marinara sauce. Top with drumsticks. Sprinkle with freshly grated Parmigiano-Reggiano cheese, if desired.

4 servings.

CHICKEN WITH ONION-APPLE SAUCE

Dzhangirova A. Svetlana
Seattle, Washington

1 (2½- to 3-lb.) broiler-fryer chicken,
  cut up
1 tablespoon olive oil
¼ teaspoon salt
¼ teaspoon freshly ground pepper
2 medium onions, chopped
3 green apples, cored, cubed
2 tablespoons fresh lemon juice
1 cup white wine
1 cinnamon stick
1 tablespoon freshly grated ginger
1 teaspoon grated anise seed, if
  desired
1 teaspoon curry powder
⅔ cup heavy cream
2 tablespoons grated lemon peel

1. Rinse chicken and pat dry.

2. In large skillet, heat oil over medium-high heat until hot. Cook chicken 20 minutes, turning occasionally, or until browned and no longer pink in center. Season with ⅛ teaspoon of the salt and ⅛ teaspoon of the pepper. Transfer to platter; keep warm.

3. For sauce, combine onions and apples in medium saucepan; sprinkle with lemon juice. Stir in wine and cinnamon stick; cover and cook over low heat 20 minutes.

4. Remove cinnamon; refrigerate until cooled. Place onion-apple mixture in blender or food processor. Add ginger, anise seed, curry and remaining ⅛ teaspoon pepper; cover and blend until smooth.

5. In medium bowl, beat cream at medium speed until soft peaks form. Stir in onion-apple mixture; season with lemon peel and remaining ⅛ teaspoon salt. Serve sauce separately.

6 servings.

QUAIL WITH HERBS

Eleanor Miller
Mount Olive, Illinois

5 tablespoons butter
4 chicken livers
½ teaspoon dried thyme
½ teaspoon dried rosemary
⅛ teaspoon salt
⅛ teaspoon freshly ground pepper
4 quail
4 strips bacon

1. Heat oven to 450°F. Spray 3-quart casserole with nonstick cooking spray.

2. In large skillet, melt 3 tablespoons of the butter over medium heat. Sauté livers until golden brown. Remove skillet from heat; stir in thyme, rosemary, salt and pepper.

3. Rinse quails and pat dry. Stuff each quail with spoonful of liver mixture. Secure legs close to body.

4. Melt remaining 2 tablespoons butter in same skillet; pour over quail. Arrange quail in casserole; top with bacon strips. Bake 20 minutes or until no longer pink in center and bacon is crisp. Serve on toasted French bread slices, surrounded with mushrooms sautéed in butter, garlic and minced scallions, if desired.

4 servings.

Stuffed Cornish Game Hens

STUFFED CORNISH GAME HENS

David A. Heppner
Brandon, Florida

1 tablespoon olive oil
1 cup chopped onion
1 teaspoon minced garlic
1^1/$_2$ cups shiitake mushrooms, stems
   removed, sliced
^{1}/$_2$ cup chopped Canadian bacon
^{1}/$_4$ cup brown long-grain rice
^{1}/$_4$ cup wild rice
1 cup reduced-sodium chicken broth
2 (10-oz.) pkg. frozen chopped
   spinach, thawed, squeezed dry
2 tablespoons slivered almonds,
   toasted
^{1}/$_4$ teaspoon salt
^{1}/$_4$ teaspoon freshly ground pepper
4 (1-lb.) Cornish game hens

1. To make stuffing, heat oil in large skillet over medium-high heat until hot. Sauté onion and garlic 5 minutes or until onion is transparent. Add mushrooms and bacon; cook, stirring often, 3 to 4 minutes or until mushrooms are wilted. Add rice; stir to coat. Add broth and increase heat to high; bring mixture to a boil. Reduce heat to low; cover and simmer 45 minutes or until rice is tender. Remove skillet from heat; stir in spinach, almonds, salt and pepper. Transfer mixture to large bowl. Stuffing may be prepared up to 2 days ahead. Refrigerate tightly covered. Stuff hens just before baking.

2. Rinse hens and pat dry. Pack each cavity with about ^{3}/$_4$ cup chilled stuffing mixture. Place breast side up on rack in roasting pan. Bake, uncovered, 45 to 55 minutes or until internal temperature reaches 180°F. Remove pan from oven; let stand 5 to 10 minutes before serving.

4 servings.

CHICKEN SOUP & DUMPLINGS

Janice Goodner
Macomb, Oklahoma

SOUP
1 (3-lb.) broiler-fryer chicken, cut up
8 cups water
2 teaspoons salt
2 teaspoons poultry seasoning
2 ribs celery, sliced
^{1}/$_8$ teaspoon freshly ground pepper
1 cup sliced carrots
1 cup cubed potatoes
2 teaspoons chicken bouillon granules

DUMPLINGS
1^1/$_2$ cups all-purpose flour
2 teaspoons baking powder
^{1}/$_2$ teaspoon salt
^{1}/$_2$ teaspoon poultry seasoning, if
   desired
3 tablespoons butter
^{1}/$_4$ cup chopped fresh parsley
^{3}/$_4$ cup reduced-sodium chicken broth,
   cooled

1. In Dutch oven, heat water to a boil over high heat. Simmer chicken and 1 teaspoon of the salt over medium-low heat 1 hour. Remove chicken; discard all fat and bones. Cut chicken into 1-inch pieces; return chicken to Dutch oven. Add poultry seasoning, celery, pepper, carrots, potatoes and chicken bouillon to water; cook over medium heat 20 minutes or until vegetables are tender.

2. To make dumplings, in large bowl, combine flour, baking powder, salt and poultry seasoning; mix until blended. Cut butter into flour mixture with pastry cutter until mixture crumbles. Stir in parsley. Quickly stir in broth. Drop dough by spoonfuls into hot chicken stew. Cook, uncovered, 10 minutes. Cook, covered, an additional 10 minutes.

6 servings.

ROASTED CHICKEN UNDER WALNUT SAUCE

Dzhangirova A. Svetlana
Seattle, Washington

1 (3-lb.) broiler-fryer chicken
$1/4$ teaspoon salt
$1/4$ teaspoon freshly ground pepper
2 medium onions, chopped
$2^1/2$ cups walnuts
2 teaspoons minced garlic
1 teaspoon ground coriander
1 tablespoon all-purpose flour
$2^1/2$ cups reduced-sodium chicken
    broth
$1/2$ teaspoon each cinnamon, ground
    cloves, ground saffrom
1 teaspoon fresh lemon juice or vinegar

1. Heat oven to 375°F. Rinse chicken and pat dry. Rub $1/8$ teaspoon of the salt inside body cavity. Skewer neck skin to back; tie legs to tail. Twist wings under back. Place breast side up on rack in shallow roasting pan. Season with remaining $1/8$ teaspoon salt and $1/8$ teaspoon of the pepper. Bake, uncovered, $1^1/4$ to $1^1/2$ hours, basting with drippings until tender and internal temperature reaches 180°F. Transfer chicken to serving platter and refrigerate.

2. Remove excess pan drippings to large measuring cup; remove and reserve fat. In medium skillet, heat half of the reserved chicken fat over medium-high heat until hot. Fry onion in skillet until tender and light brown. Set aside. In mortar or bowl, pound nuts with garlic, remaining $1/8$ teaspoon pepper and coriander. Set aside.

3. Pour remaining chicken fat into large skillet; stir in flour. Add broth to flour mixture and cook over medium heat until thickened and bubbly. Stir in walnut mixture and onion; cook and stir an additional 1 minute. Add cinnamon, cloves, saffron and lemon juice; cook over low heat 5 minutes. Remove chicken from refrigerator. Cut chicken into serving pieces; place on serving platter and top with hot sauce to cover. Let cool. Serve cold.

4 to 6 servings.

CHIPOTLE ONION CHICKEN

David Lee Summers
Las Cruces, New Mexico

1 tablespoon sugar
2 teaspoons garlic powder
2 teaspoons dried parsley
1 teaspoon chipotle chile powder
1 teaspoon ancho chile powder
1 teaspoon ground cumin
1 teaspoon onion powder
3 tablespoons all-purpose flour
8 chicken pieces (about $3^1/2$ lb.)
2 tablespoons vegetable oil
$1/2$ cup chopped onion
4 cups reduced-sodium chicken broth
3 tablespoons chipotle paste

1. In small bowl, combine sugar, garlic powder, parsley, chile powders, cumin and onion powder. In medium bowl, combine flour with 2 tablespoons of the sugar seasoning.

2. Rinse chicken and pat dry. Sprinkle seasoning over chicken pieces; rub in well.

3. In Dutch oven, heat oil over high heat until oil begins to smoke. Brown chicken in batches, about 2 to 3 minutes per side. Remove chicken and set aside.

4. Add onions to pot; cook, stirring and scraping occasionally, until onions are brown. Add $1/2$ cup broth, chipotle paste and seasoned flour. Continue to cook until flour begins to stick. Stir in remaining broth; scrape bottom of pot well. Return chicken and pan juices to pot, then bring to a boil.

5. Reduce heat to low and simmer about 30 minutes or until chicken is tender and no longer pink in center. Remove from heat and serve.

4 to 6 servings.

BUTTERMILK CHICKEN
Marsha Kay Clow–Crookston, Minnesota

1/4 cup butter
1 (3- to 4-lb.) broiler-fryer chicken, cut up
1 1/2 cups buttermilk
3/4 cup all-purpose flour
1 1/2 teaspoons salt
1/4 teaspoon freshly ground pepper
1 (10 3/4-oz.) can condensed cream of chicken soup

1. Heat oven to 375°F. In oven, melt butter in 13x9-inch pan.

2. Rinse chicken and pat dry. Pour 1/2 cup of the buttermilk into shallow bowl. In medium bowl, combine flour, salt and pepper; mix well. Dip chicken in flour mixture, buttermilk, then in flour mixture again. Arrange chicken skin side down in pan.

3. Bake 30 minutes; turn chicken over and bake an additional 15 minutes. Drain fat.

4. In another medium bowl, combine remaining 1 cup buttermilk and soup; mix well. Pour over chicken; bake an additional 15 minutes or until chicken is no longer pink in center.

4 to 6 servings.

BROCCOLI-STUFFED CHICKEN
Debbie Patt–Holley, New York

CHICKEN
4 (1-lb.) boneless skinless chicken breast halves, butterflied
1/2 cup (2 oz.) shredded cheddar cheese
3/4 cup chopped fresh broccoli
1/8 teaspoon salt
1/8 teaspoon freshly ground pepper
1/2 teaspoon dried basil
2 teaspoons freshly grated Parmesan cheese
1 cup dry bread crumbs
1 egg, beaten

BROCCOLI SAUCE
1/2 cup chopped fresh broccoli
1/2 cup reduced-sodium chicken broth
1/4 cup heavy cream
1/4 teaspoon dried basil
1/4 teaspoon dried oregano
1/4 teaspoon salt
1/4 teaspoon freshly ground pepper

1. Heat oven to 350°F. Spray 8-inch square pan with nonstick cooking spray.

2. Rinse chicken and pat dry. Stuff each chicken pocket with 1 tablespoon cheddar cheese and 2 tablespoons broccoli florets. Season with salt, pepper and dash of basil. Secure chicken with toothpicks. In shallow dish, mix Parmesan and bread crumbs. Place egg in another shallow dish. Dip each chicken piece into egg, then roll in bread crumbs.

3. Arrange chicken breasts in pan 1 inch apart. Bake 30 minutes or until chicken juices run clear. During last few minutes of baking, sprinkle remaining cheddar cheese over chicken.

4. To make sauce, puree broccoli in food processor. Combine puree, broth, cream, basil, oregano, salt and pepper in large saucepan. Simmer 10 minutes, stirring frequently, until sauce thickens. Serve over chicken. Garnish with parsley and chives.

4 servings.

SPICED CHICKEN RICE AND AVOCADO

Cheryl Bullard
Littleton, Colorado

1 (6.9-oz.) pkg. chicken rice mix
1 (5-oz.) can chunk chicken, drained
1 (4-oz.) can diced green chiles, drained
1 1/2 cups (6 oz.) shredded jalapeño Monterey Jack cheese
3 avocados, halved, pitted
1 1/2 cups tomato salsa

1. Cook chicken rice mix according to package directions. Add chicken and chiles to saucepan; heat through. Add cheese; heat until melted.

2. For each serving, slice one avocado half; top with rice mixture and salsa.

4 to 6 servings.

COLA BARBECUE CHICKEN

Marianne Lavella
Lady Lake, Florida

1 (3-lb.) broiler-fryer chicken, cut up
1 cup ketchup
2 cups carbonated cola beverage

1. Rinse chicken and pat dry. In medium bowl, combine ketchup and cola. Pour into 250°F electric frying pan. Cover and simmer chicken, stirring occasionally 1 to 1 1/2 hours, or until sauce is thick and chicken is no longer pink in center.

4 servings.

ALGERIAN CHICKEN COUSCOUS

Vivian Nikanow
Chicago, Illinois

2 tablespoons olive oil
1 medium onion, sliced, separated into rings
2 garlic cloves, minced
1 (3-lb.) broiler-fryer chicken, cut up
1 (16-oz.) can diced tomatoes
2 medium carrots, cut into 1-inch pieces
1 rib celery, sliced
1 medium turnip, peeled, cubed
1/2 teaspoon salt
1 medium zucchini, cut into 1/2-inch pieces
1/2 cup raisins
2 tablespoons water
4 teaspoons cornstarch
1 1/2 cups couscous
3 tablespoons chopped fresh parsley

1. In large saucepan, heat oil over medium-high heat until hot. Sauté onion and garlic until onion is transparent. Remove garlic and onions from skillet; set aside. Rinse chicken and pat dry. Add chicken to saucepan; cook over medium heat 15 minutes. Remove fat.

2. Return onion and garlic to saucepan; add tomatoes, carrots, celery, turnip and salt. Bring to a boil. Reduce heat, cover and simmer 30 minutes. Stir in zucchini and raisins; cover and simmer an additional 15 minutes or until vegetables are tender. Skim off fat.

3. In small bowl, whisk together water and cornstarch; stir into tomato mixture. Cook and stir until thickened and bubbly. Cook and stir an additional 2 minutes.

4. Meanwhile, prepare couscous according to package directions; stir in parsley.

5. Serve chicken over couscous. Top with onion mixture.

6 servings.

Algerian Chicken Couscous

TANGO MANGO CHICKEN

Nancy Suske
Kailua, Hawaii

2 (¹/₂-lb.) boneless skinless chicken
    breast halves
¹/₄ cup plus 2 tablespoons red wine
    vinegar
¹/₂ teaspoon dried thyme
¹/₄ cup packed brown sugar
1 teaspoon minced fresh ginger
1 garlic clove, chopped
1 tablespoon chopped onion
1 mango, diced
¹/₈ teaspoon salt
¹/₈ teaspoon freshly ground pepper

1. Heat oven to 325°F. Spray 3-quart casserole with nonstick cooking spray.

2. Rinse chicken and pat dry. Place chicken in glass bowl.

3. In small bowl, combine ¹/₄ cup of the vinegar and thyme; mix well. Pour mixture over chicken and refrigerate 2 hours, turning occasionally.

4. In small saucepan, combine brown sugar, ginger, garlic, onion and remaining 2 tablespoons vinegar. Add mango; bring to a boil over medium heat, stirring occasionally.

5. Remove chicken from marinade and place in casserole; discard marinade. Season with salt and pepper. Bake 50 minutes or until chicken is no longer pink in center. Remove chicken from pan and keep warm.

6. Return sugar mixture to a boil over medium heat. Stir and cook about 4 minutes or until slightly thickened. Pour sauce over chicken. Serve with rice.

2 servings.

CRUNCHY CHICKEN ALMONDINE

Debbie Patt
Holley, New York

3 (1-lb.) boneless skinless chicken
    breast halves
5 cups crushed corn flakes cereal
³/₄ cup slivered ground almonds
¹/₈ teaspoon salt
1 egg
1 cup milk
1 teaspoon almond extract
1 cup all-purpose flour
¹/₈ teaspoon freshly ground pepper

1. Heat oven to 350°F. Spray 13x9-inch pan with nonstick cooking spray.

2. Rinse chicken and pat dry. Place each chicken breast between 2 sheets parchment paper; pound until ¹/₂ inch thick. Repeat with remaining breasts.

3. In medium bowl, combine corn flakes, almonds and dash of salt; mix well. Set aside.

4. In another medium bowl, beat egg, milk and almond extract at medium speed until frothy. Add flour, salt and pepper; continue beating until smooth.

5. Dip chicken into batter, then coat with corn flake-almond mixture. Arrange chicken pieces in pan about 1 inch apart. Bake, uncovered, 45 minutes or until internal temperature reaches 160°F. Serve while hot and crunchy.

6 servings.

LEMON HERBED CHICKEN

Nikole L. Braue
Pontiac, Michigan

4 (1-lb.) boneless skinless chicken
   breast halves
$1^1/_2$ teaspoons seasoned salt
$1^1/_2$ teaspoons garlic powder
$1^1/_2$ teaspoons herbes de Provence
$^1/_3$ cup mayonnaise
1 lemon, halved, seeded, juice
   reserved
$1^1/_2$ tablespoons all-purpose flour

1. Heat oven to 425°F. Spray 13x9-inch pan with nonstick cooking spray.

2. Rinse chicken and pat dry; set aside.

3. In small bowl, combine seasoned salt, garlic powder, herbes de Provence, mayonnaise, lemon juice and flour; mix well.

4. Arrange chicken breasts in pan about 1 inch apart. Brush tops of chicken with half of the lemon-herb sauce; bake 10 minutes. Turn chicken and brush with remaining sauce; bake an additional 12 to15 minutes or until chicken is no longer pink in center. Garnish with rosemary or parsley.

4 servings.

AUNT ANNE'S PINEAPPLE CHICKEN

Susan M. Bork
Indianapolis, Indiana

4 (1-lb.) boneless skinless chicken
   breast halves
$^1/_8$ teaspoon garlic powder
2 eggs, beaten
$^1/_2$ cup all-purpose flour
$^1/_2$ cup sugar
1 (8-oz.) can pineapple chunks,
   drained, $^1/_4$ cup pineapple juice
   reserved
$^3/_4$ cup white vinegar
$^3/_4$ cup ketchup
1 teaspoon low-sodium soy sauce
$^3/_4$ teaspoon salt

1. Heat oven to 350°F. Spray 13x9-inch pan with nonstick cooking spray.

2. Rinse chicken and pat dry. Season chicken breasts with garlic powder. Dip breasts in egg, then in flour to coat. Arrange chicken breasts in pan about 1 inch apart.

3. In medium saucepan, stir together sugar, pineapple juice, vinegar, ketchup, soy sauce and salt. Bring to a boil. Pour mixture over chicken. Arrange pineapple around chicken.

4. Bake, uncovered, 20 to 25 minutes or until internal temperature reaches 160°F. Serve with salad and French bread.

4 servings.

Baked Chicken with Oranges, Apricots & Dried Cranberries

BAKED CHICKEN WITH ORANGES, APRICOTS & DRIED CRANBERRIES

Charlotte Ward
Hilton Head Island, South Carolina

6 boneless skinless chicken breast
   halves (about 1$^1/_2$ lb.)
$^1/_4$ cup minced onion
$^1/_4$ cup paprika
$^1/_2$ teaspoon salt
$^1/_4$ teaspoon rosemary
$^1/_4$ teaspoon freshly ground pepper
$^1/_2$ cup minced dried apricots
$^1/_2$ cup dried cranberries
1 (11-oz.) can mandarin oranges,
   drained
2 tablespoons all-purpose flour
2 cups fresh orange juice
1 teaspoon dried grated orange peel
2 tablespoons orange-flavored liqueur

1. Heat oven to 350°F. Spray 3-quart casserole with nonstick cooking spray.

2. Rinse chicken and pat dry. Arrange chicken in casserole about 1 inch apart. Sprinkle with onion, paprika, salt, rosemary, pepper, apricots, cranberries and oranges.

3. In medium bowl, whisk together flour and $^1/_2$ cup of the orange juice; mix well. Stir in orange peel, liqueur and remaining 1$^1/_2$ cups orange juice. Pour mixture over chicken.

4. Bake, uncovered, 45 minutes or until chicken is no longer pink in center. Baste every 15 minutes. Remove chicken and cut into 1-inch-thick strips. Place strips over rice or angel hair pasta and top with sauce.

6 servings.

CHICKEN LIVERS STROGANOFF

Charlotte Ward
Hilton Head Island, South Carolina

1 tablespoon vegetable oil
1 medium onion, chopped
6 oz. sliced fresh mushrooms
$^1/_2$ lb. chicken livers
1 tablespoon all-purpose flour
2 tablespoons ketchup
$^1/_4$ cup white wine
2 tablespoons reduced-sodium chicken
   broth
$^1/_4$ teaspoon salt
$^1/_8$ teaspoon freshly ground pepper
$^1/_4$ teaspoon ground mace
$^1/_2$ cup sour cream or plain yogurt
1 tablespoon fresh chopped dill or 1
   teaspoon dried

1. In large saucepan, heat oil over medium heat until hot. Sauté onions until transparent Add mushrooms; sauté 3 to 4 minutes or until soft. Add chicken livers; brown 6 to 8 minutes or until no longer pink in center.

2. In medium bowl, combine flour, ketchup, wine, broth, salt and pepper; mix well. Pour mixture into saucepan. Cover and simmer 10 minutes. Stir in mace, sour cream and dill; toss gently. Heat through and serve over brown rice.

2 servings.

CRISPY BAKED CHICKEN BREASTS

Joan O'Brien
Charlestown, Rhode Island

6 (1½ lb.) boneless skinless chicken
   breast halves
2 cups sour cream
4 teaspoons Worcestershire sauce
2 teaspoons paprika
¼ cup fresh lemon juice
2 teaspoons celery salt
2 garlic cloves, finely chopped
1 teaspoon salt
½ teaspoon freshly ground pepper
1⅓ cups dry bread crumbs
2 tablespoons butter, melted
2 tablespoons vegetable oil

1. Rinse chicken and pat dry. Place chicken in large resealable plastic bag.

2. In large bowl, combine sour cream, Worcestershire sauce, paprika, lemon juice, celery salt, garlic, salt and pepper; mix well. Pour over chicken. Seal bag; cover and refrigerate overnight.

3. Heat oven to 350°F. Spray 8-inch square pan with nonstick cooking spray.

4. Remove chicken from marinade; discard marinade. Roll chicken in bread crumbs. Place chicken in pan.

5. In small bowl, combine butter and oil; mix well. Pour half of the butter mixture over chicken. Bake, uncovered, 30 minutes or until chicken is no longer pink in center. Remove from oven and pour remaining half butter mixture over chicken. Bake an additional 10 minutes.

6 servings.

CHICKEN CARLOTTA

Charlotte Ward
Hilton Head Island,
South Carolina

2 (½-lb.) boneless skinless chicken
   breast halves
1 tablespoon olive oil
½ lb. fresh mushrooms, sliced
3 garlic cloves, minced
2 tablespoons capers
1 (14-oz.) can artichoke hearts,
   quartered
1 cup dry white wine
½ cup diced fresh tomatoes
2 tablespoons fresh lemon juice
¼ cup chopped green onions
1 teaspoon dried dill
¼ teaspoon cinnamon
⅛ teaspoon nutmeg

1. Rinse chicken and pat dry. In large skillet, heat oil over medium-high heat until hot. Sauté chicken until lightly browned and no longer pink in center. Remove chicken from skillet.

2. In large bowl, combine mushrooms, garlic, capers and artichoke hearts; mix well. Pour mixture into skillet. Stir in wine, tomatoes, lemon juice, onions, dill, cinnamon and nutmeg. Simmer, uncovered, until sauce thickens.

3. Return chicken to skillet and heat through. Serve over brown rice and sprinkle with feta cheese.

4 servings.

CHICKEN IN PEAR SAUCE

Tammy Raynes
Natchitoches, Louisiana

4 (1-lb.) boneless skinless chicken
   breast halves
$1/2$ teaspoon salt
$1/8$ teaspoon freshly ground pepper
2 tablespoons vegetable oil
5 thick slices bacon
1 (14.5-oz.) can reduced-sodium
   chicken broth
3 medium ripe pears, peeled, diced
2 tablespoons cornstarch
2 tablespoons cold water
$1/4$ cup chopped fresh chives

1. Rinse chicken and pat dry. Season with salt and pepper.

2. In large skillet, heat oil over medium-high heat until hot. Cook chicken 10 minutes per side or until no longer pink in center. Keep warm.

3. Meanwhile, cook bacon in another large skillet until crisp. Drain, reserving 1 tablespoon drippings; set bacon aside.

4. Gradually stir broth into bacon drippings, scraping pan to loosen browned bits. Bring to a boil and cook, uncovered, 5 minutes. Add pears; return to a boil and cook an additional 5 minutes or until pears are tender.

5. In small bowl, whisk together cornstarch and water until smooth; add chives. Gradually stir into pear sauce; bring to a boil. Cook and stir 2 minutes or until thickened and bubbly. Stir in bacon. Pour mixture over chicken.

4 servings.

TOMATO-BASIL RISOTTO

Kimberlee Wilson
Albany, Georgia

3 lb. chicken breast tenderloins
2 tablespoons butter
2 large Italian sausage links, sliced
1 large onion, chopped
1 large green bell pepper, chopped
1 large garlic clove, minced
3 cups hot cooked rice
1 (14.5-oz.) can stewed tomatoes
4 cups reduced-sodium chicken broth
1 tablespoon dried basil
$1/8$ teaspoon salt
$1/8$ teaspoon freshly ground pepper
1 cup heavy cream

1. Rinse chicken and pat dry. In Dutch oven, melt butter over medium-low heat. Sauté chicken, sausage, onion, bell pepper and garlic until chicken is no longer pink in center. Stir in rice, tomatoes, broth, basil, salt and pepper; bring to a boil. Cover and reduce heat; simmer 20 minutes, stirring occasionally. When water is completely absorbed, stir in cream. Cook on low heat, stirring frequently, an additional 5 minutes.

6 to 8 servings.

TACO-SEASONED CHICKEN AND BEANS

Tammy Raynes
Natchitoches, Louisiana

2 cups water
1 (1-oz.) pkg. taco seasoning mix
$1/4$ teaspoon salt
1 cup long-grain white rice
1 (15-oz.) can black beans, drained
1 tablespoon olive oil
1 lb. boneless skinless chicken breast
    halves, cut into thin strips
1 (14.5-oz.) can Mexican-flavored
    stewed tomatoes
$3/4$ cup frozen corn kernels, thawed
1 tablespoon fresh lime juice

1. In medium saucepan, combine water, 1 teaspoon of the taco seasoning, salt and rice. Bring to a boil, stirring well. Cover and reduce heat to low. Cook 20 minutes; let stand 5 minutes. Rinse beans and drain again.

2. In large skillet, heat oil over medium-high heat until hot. Sauté chicken 2 minutes, just until strips begin to whiten. Sprinkle remaining taco seasoning over chicken and cook an additional 1 minute. Add tomatoes and simmer 4 minutes. Stir in beans and corn; simmer 5 minutes until chicken is no longer pink in center. Stir in lime juice. Fluff rice with fork. Spoon chicken and sauce over rice.

4 servings.

TURKEY WITH FRUITS

Dzhangirova A. Svetlana
Seattle, Washington

4 tablespoons olive oil
4 cored sliced pears
$1/2$ cup reduced-sodium chicken broth
$1/2$ cup white wine
1 lb. boneless turkey breast halves
$1/8$ teaspoon salt
$1/8$ teaspoon freshly ground pepper
1 teaspoon curry powder
1 tablespoon cornstarch
1 bunch green onions, sliced
$2/3$ cup heavy cream

1. In large skillet, heat 2 tablespoons of the oil over medium heat until hot. Braise pears 5 minutes. Stir in broth and wine; cook an additional 5 minutes. Set aside.

2. Wash turkey and pat dry. Cut into 1-inch-thick strips. Season with salt, pepper and curry powder; roll in cornstarch.

3. Heat remaining 2 tablespoons oil in another large skillet. Cook turkey until light brown. Stir in onion; braise with turkey 5 minutes. Stir in pear mixture and cream; cook an additional 5 minutes until inernal temperature reaches 180°F. Season with salt and pepper. Serve over hot cooked rice or noodles.

4 servings.

Turkey with Fruits

CHICKEN FAJITAS

Karie Hansen
Fairfield, Iowa

2 tablespoons olive oil
1 red bell pepper, chopped
1 green bell pepper, chopped
1 yellow bell pepper, chopped
¼ cup chopped red onion
1 teaspoon dried oregano
1 teaspoon dried basil
2 teaspoons crushed red pepper
3 boneless skinless chicken breast
   halves, cut into thin strips
1 (16-oz.) pkg. flour tortillas
1 cup (4 oz.) shredded cheddar
   cheese
1 (12-oz.) jar hot salsa
1 (8-oz.) container sour cream
1 (12-oz.) jar guacamole

1. In large skillet, heat oil over medium-high heat until hot. Sauté bell peppers and onion until onion is transparent. Season with oregano, basil and red pepper. Add chicken; cook about 5 minutes or until chicken is no longer pink in center.

2. Serve mixture wrapped in warm tortillas. Serve with cheese, salsa, sour cream and guacamole.

3 to 4 servings.

SESAME CHICKEN

Tammy Raynes
Natchitoches, Louisiana

2 teaspoons vegetable oil
1 boneless skinless chicken breast
   half, cut into 1-inch strips
7 snow pea pods
1 cup broccoli florets
1 red bell pepper, coarsely chopped
3 medium fresh mushrooms, sliced
¾ cup chopped onion
1 tablespoon cornstarch
1 teaspoon sugar
½ cup cold water
3 to 4 tablespoons low-sodium soy
   sauce
Hot cooked rice
1 teaspoon toasted sesame seeds

1. In wok, heat oil over medium-high heat until hot. Stir-fry chicken 6 to 8 minutes or until no longer pink in center. Remove chicken and set aside. In same wok, stir-fry peas, broccoli and bell pepper 2 to 3 minutes or until softened. Add mushrooms and onion; stir-fry 3 to 4 minutes or until softened.

2. In medium saucepan, combine cornstarch and sugar; stir in water and soy sauce. Bring to a boil; cook 1 to 2 minutes or until thickened. Pour over vegetables in wok.

3. Return chicken to wok; cook until heated through and vegetables are tender. Serve chicken over rice. Sprinkle with sesame seeds.

2 servings.

PERFECT PASTA

SPAGHETTI

Ginger Heitman
Camp Point, Illinois

1/2 lb. thick-sliced bacon, cut into
   1/2-inch pieces
1 medium onion, chopped
4 cups tomatoes, seeded, chopped
3 tablespoons sugar
1/8 teaspoon salt
1/8 teaspoon freshly ground pepper
1/4 teaspoon ground cloves
1 tablespoon kosher (coarse) salt
1 (7-oz.) pkg. spaghetti

1. In large skillet, fry bacon over medium-high heat until crisp; drain fat. Sauté onion 4 minutes. Add tomatoes, sugar, salt, pepper and cloves; mix well and simmer 20 minutes.

2. Fill large pot two-thirds full of water; add 1 tablespoon salt. Bring to a boil over high heat. Cook spaghetti according to package directions. Rinse and drain spaghetti thoroughly in cool water.

3. Transfer spaghetti to large bowl; pour hot sauce over spaghetti. Sprinkle with freshly grated Parmesan cheese, if desired.

4 to 6 servings.

GLORIFIED SPAGHETTI

Valerie Hobbs
Deerfield, Illinois

2 tablespoons butter
1 1/2 lb. ground beef
1 lb. mushrooms, sliced
1 (15-oz.) can tomato sauce
1 (6-oz.) can tomato paste
1 teaspoon dried basil
1 teaspoon dried oregano
1/8 teaspoon salt
1/8 teaspoon freshly ground pepper
1 cup cottage cheese
1 (8-oz.) pkg. cream cheese, cut into
   1-inch pieces
1/2 cup chopped green onions
1/2 cup chopped green bell pepper
1 (8-oz.) container sour cream
1 tablespoon kosher (coarse) salt
1 (12-oz.) pkg. spaghetti

1. Spray 3-quart casserole with nonstick cooking spray.

2. In large skillet, melt butter over medium heat. Cook beef until no longer pink in center. Stir in mushrooms, tomato sauce, tomato paste, basil, oregano, salt and pepper.

3. In large bowl, combine cottage cheese, cream cheese, green onion, bell pepper and sour cream; mix gently.

4. Fill large pot two-thirds full of water; add 1 tablespoon salt. Bring to a boil over high heat. Cook spaghetti according to package directions. Rinse and drain spaghetti thoroughly in cool water. Add spaghetti and meat mixtures to cottage cheese mixture. Toss gently, but thoroughly. Pour mixture into casserole. Refrigerate overnight.

5. Heat oven to 350°F. Bake, covered, 20 minutes. Remove cover; bake an additional 35 minutes.

12 servings.

STEPHANIE'S SCRUMPTIOUS SPAGHETTI SAUCE

Stephanie Goodall
Citrus Heights, California

1 lb. ground beef
1 medium onion, chopped
2 garlic cloves, minced
1 (14.5-oz.) can Italian tomato sauce
1 (14.5-oz.) can whole peeled
  tomatoes
2 (6-oz.) cans tomato paste
1 (8-oz.) can mushroom stems
$1/2$ cup red wine
2 tablespoons fresh chopped basil
2 tablespoons fresh chopped oregano
$1/2$ teaspoon freshly ground pepper

1. In large skillet, cook beef over medium-high heat until no longer pink in center. Add onion and garlic to skillet. Sauté until onion is transparent; drain well.

2. Combine tomato sauce, tomatoes, tomato paste and mushrooms in slow cooker set on high heat setting. Stir in beef, onion and garlic; mix well. Add wine, basil, oregano and pepper. Heat sauce to a simmer. Reduce heat to low setting and cook 8 hours.

8 servings.

MOMMA'S SPAGGY SAUCE AND PASTA

Vicki Schuler
Atlantic, Iowa

1 tablespoon kosher (coarse) salt
1 (7-oz.) pkg. spaghetti
2 tablespoons olive oil
1 large yellow onion, chopped
1 medium green bell pepper, chopped
2 to 3 large garlic cloves, minced
4 cups canned whole tomatoes
2 (8-oz.) cans tomato sauce
2 tablespoons chopped fresh basil
1 tablespoon chopped fresh oregano
$1/2$ teaspoon salt
$1/4$ teaspoon freshly ground pepper

1. Fill large pot two-thirds full of water; add 1 tablespoon salt. Bring to a boil over high heat. Cook spaghetti according to package directions. Rinse and drain spaghetti thoroughly in cool water. Set aside.

2. In medium skillet, heat oil over medium-high heat until hot. Sauté onion and bell pepper 3 minutes or until onion is transparent.

3. Stir in garlic, tomatoes, tomato sauce, basil, oregano, salt and pepper; mix well, breaking up tomatoes. Heat to a boil, then reduce heat to low. Cover and simmer 45 minutes.

4. In large bowl, pour hot sauce over spaghetti. Sprinkle with freshly grated Parmesan cheese, if desired.

4 cups.

Spaghetti à la Bentley

SPAGHETTI A LA BENTLEY

Ren Evans
Baltimore, Maryland

$^1/_2$ cup butter
$1^1/_2$ large onions, chopped
2 green bell peppers, chopped
1 teaspoon garlic salt
$^1/_2$ tablespoon garlic powder
2 lb. ground beef
$^1/_2$ tablespoon dried oregano
1 tablespoon kosher (coarse) salt
2 (8-oz.) pkg. angel hair pasta
6 Italian hot sausages
1 (6-oz.) can tomato paste
4 (15-oz.) cans tomato sauce
3 (15-oz.) cans Italian tomato sauce
1 (28-oz.) can whole tomatoes, cut
    into thirds
4 bay leaves
1 teaspoon freshly ground pepper
1 lb. sliced mushrooms

1. In large skillet, melt butter over medium-high heat. Sauté onions, bell peppers, $^1/_4$ teaspoon of the garlic salt and $^1/_2$ teaspoon of the garlic powder until onions are transparent. Add ground beef, keeping onion mixture to outside. Stir in oregano. Cook mixture until beef is no longer pink in center, turning and mixing several times. Drain in colander. Set aside.

2. In large pot, boil sausages in water 10 to 12 minutes. Add ground beef mixture, tomato paste, sauces, whole tomatoes, bay leaves, pepper and mushrooms. Simmer about 6 hours or until reduced approximately 1 inch. Discard bay leaves. Serve over pasta.

3. Fill another large pot two-thirds full of water; add 1 tablespoon salt. Bring to a boil over high heat. Cook angel hair pasta according to package directions; drain. Serve sauce over pasta.

12 servings.

CHICKEN ALFREDO

Rose L. Davis
Clinton, Connecticut

CHICKEN
4 (1-lb.) boneless skinless chicken
    breasts halves, cut into 1-inch
    pieces
$1^1/_2$ teaspoons seasoned salt
$^1/_2$ teaspoon garlic powder
$^1/_2$ teaspoon freshly ground pepper
$^1/_2$ teaspoon crushed dried basil
$^1/_2$ teaspoon crushed dried oregano
$^1/_4$ teaspoon dried parsley

SAUCE
3 tablespoons all-purpose flour
1 to $1^1/_2$ tablespoons margarine
$^1/_2$ cup half-and-half
$^1/_2$ cup nonfat milk
4 oz. fresh mushrooms, chopped
$^1/_2$ cup frozen baby peas
1 tablespoon kosher (coarse) salt
1 (8-oz.) pkg. fettuccine
$^1/_2$ cup (2 oz.) freshly grated
    Parmesan cheese

1. Rinse chicken and pat dry.

2. Spray large skillet with nonstick cooking spray. Add chicken, salt, garlic powder, pepper, basil, oregano and parsley. Cook over medium-high heat, stirring constantly, until chicken is no longer pink in center.

3. Add flour and margarine to skillet; stir 3 to 5 minutes or until margarine is melted. Remove skillet from heat.

4. Stir in half-and-half, milk, mushrooms and peas. Return skillet to heat; bring to a boil. Reduce heat to low; cook until sauce is thick and bubbly. Remove from heat; set aside.

5. Fill large pot two-thirds full of water; add 1 tablespoon salt. Bring to a boil over high heat. Cook fettuccine according to package directions; drain. Do not rinse. Stir fettuccine and cheese into skillet. Warm thoroughly; toss until well coated.

4 to 6 servings.

ZUCCHINI-BEEF LASAGNA

Tammy Raynes
Natchitoches, Louisiana

1 tablespoon kosher (coarse) salt
16 oz. lasagna noodles
1 lb. lean ground beef
2 garlic cloves, minced
2 (8-oz.) cans tomato sauce
$1/2$ cup water
1 (6-oz.) can tomato paste
2 bay leaves
1 teaspoon minced fresh parsley
1 teaspoon dried Italian seasoning
1 cup reduced-fat cottage cheese
1 small zucchini, cooked, sliced
1 (8-oz.) container reduced-fat
   sour cream

1. Heat oven to 350°F. Spray 13x9-inch pan with nonstick cooking spray.

2. Fill large pot two-thirds full of water; add 1 tablespoon salt. Bring to a boil over high heat. Cook lasagna noodles according to package directions; drain. Set aside.

3. In large skillet, cook beef and garlic over medium heat until meat is no longer pink in center; drain. Stir in tomato sauce, water, tomato paste, bay leaves, parsley and Italian seasoning. Bring to a boil; reduce heat. Simmer, uncovered, 30 to 40 minutes. Discard bay leaves.

4. Spread $1/2$ cup meat sauce in pan. Arrange 5 noodles over sauce, cutting to fit. Spread with cottage cheese. Cover with another 5 noodles, half of the meat sauce and zucchini. Cover with another 5 noodles and sour cream. Top with remaining noodles and remaining meat sauce.

5. Bake, uncovered, 30 to 35 minutes or until heated through. Let stand 15 minutes before cutting.

12 servings.

QUICK AND EASY BROCCOLI PASTA

Debbie Patt
Holley, New York

1 tablespoon kosher (coarse) salt
1 lb. ditalini pasta
1 tablespoon olive oil
1 medium onion, chopped
2 garlic cloves
1 head broccoli, chopped
2 cups reduced-sodium chicken broth
2 tablespoons freshly grated Parmesan
   cheese

1. Fill large pot two-thirds full of water; add 1 tablespoon salt. Bring to a boil over high heat. Cook ditalini according to package directions. Rinse and drain thoroughly in cool water. Set aside.

2. Meanwhile, in large skillet, heat oil over medium-high heat until hot. Sauté onion and garlic until onion is transparent. Stir in broccoli and broth. Cook until broccoli is tender.

3. Pour vegetable mixture over ditalini. Sprinkle with freshly grated Parmesan cheese.

6 to 8 servings.

CHICKEN AND BROCCOLI ALFREDO

Jennifer Gumm
Killeen, Texas

1 tablespoon kosher (coarse) salt
1 (8-oz.) pkg. linguine
1 cup broccoli florets
2 tablespoons butter
1 lb. boneless skinless chicken breast,
  cut into $3/4$-inch pieces
1 ($10^3/4$-oz.) can condensed cream of
  mushroom soup
$1/2$ cup milk
$1/4$ teaspoon freshly ground pepper
$1/2$ cup (2 oz.) freshly grated
  Parmesan cheese

1. Fill large pot two-thirds full of water; add 1 tablespoon salt. Bring to a boil over high heat. Cook linguine according to package directions. Add broccoli during last 4 minutes of cooking time. Rinse and drain linguine thoroughly in cool water. Set aside.

2. In large skillet, melt butter over medium heat. Cook chicken until browned and no longer pink in center, stirring often. Add soup, milk, pepper, cheese and linguine; toss gently to cover. Heat thoroughly.

4 servings.

JOHNNY MOZETTI

Mary Ann Schmitt
Boonville, Indiana

1 tablespoon kosher (coarse) salt
1 (16-oz.) pkg. lasagna noodles
1 lb. ground beef
2 medium onions, chopped
4 ribs celery, sliced
2 large green bell peppers, chopped
1 (10-oz.) jar pimiento-stuffed olives
1 (4-oz.) can sliced mushrooms
1 (6-oz.) can tomato paste
2 ($10^3/4$-oz.) cans condensed tomato
  soup
$1/8$ teaspoon hot pepper sauce
1 tablespoon sugar
4 cups (16 oz.) shredded colby cheese

1. Heat oven to 350°F. Spray 13x9-inch pan with nonstick cooking spray.

2. Fill large pot two-thirds full of water; add 1 tablespoon salt. Bring to a boil over high heat. Cook lasagna noodles according to package directions; drain. Set aside.

3. In large skillet, cook beef over medium-high heat until no longer pink in center; drain. Add onion, celery, bell peppers, olives and mushrooms. Stir in tomato paste, soup, hot pepper sauce and sugar; mix until heated thoroughly.

4. Alternately layer noodles and meat mixture in pan. Bake 30 minutes; remove from oven. Sprinkle cheese over lasagna. Bake an additional 30 minutes until hot and bubbly.

12 servings.

ITALIAN-STUFFED SHELLS

Tammy Raynes
Natchitoches, Louisiana

1 tablespoon kosher (coarse) salt
24 jumbo pasta shells
1 lb. ground beef
1 cup chopped onion
1 garlic clove, minced
2 cups hot water
1 (12-oz.) can tomato paste
1 tablespoon beef bouillon granules
1½ teaspoons dried oregano
1 (16-oz.) container cottage cheese
2 cups (8 oz.) shredded mozzarella
  cheese
½ cup (2 oz.) freshly grated
  Parmesan cheese
1 egg, beaten

1. Heat oven to 350°F. Spray 13x9-inch pan with nonstick cooking spray.

2. Fill large pot two-thirds full of water; add 1 tablespoon salt. Bring to a boil over high heat. Cook pasta according to package directions; drain. Set aside.

3. In large skillet, cook beef, onion and garlic over medium-high heat until beef is no longer pink in center; drain well. Stir in water, tomato paste, bouillon and oregano; simmer, uncovered, 30 minutes.

4. Meanwhile, in medium bowl, combine cottage cheese, 1 cup of the mozzarella, Parmesan and egg; beat at medium speed until smooth.

5. Stuff shells with cheese mixture; arrange in pan. Pour meat sauce over shells. Cover and bake 30 minutes. Uncover; sprinkle with remaining 1 cup mozzarella. Bake an additional 5 minutes or until cheese is melted.

6 to 8 servings.

GINGER'S SPRINGTIME NOODLES

Peggy Winkworth
Durango, Colorado

½ lb. asparagus
¼ cup butter
½ lb. fresh mushrooms, sliced
¼ lb. slivered proscuitto or baked
  ham, if desired
1 medium carrot, thinly sliced
1 medium zucchini, chopped
1 (8-oz.) pkg. linguini
1 tablespoon kosher (coarse) salt
3 green onions, sliced (including tops)
½ cup fresh peas or frozen baby
  peas, thawed
1 teaspoon dried basil
½ teaspoon salt
Dash nutmeg
Dash white pepper
1 cup whipping cream
¼ cup (1 oz.) freshly grated
  Parmesan cheese
1 tablespoon chopped fresh parsley

1. Cut spears diagonally into 1-inch lengths, leaving tips whole.

2. In large skillet, melt butter over medium heat. Cook mushrooms, proscuitto, asparagus, carrot and zucchini 3 minutes, stirring occasionally. Cover and continue cooking an additional 1 minute.

3. Fill large pot two-thirds full of water; add 1 tablespoon salt. Bring to a boil over high heat. Cook linguine according to package directions. Rinse and drain thoroughly in cool water. Set aside.

4. Add green onions, peas, basil, salt, nutmeg, pepper and cream to vegetable mixture. Increase heat to high; cook until liquid boils all over and forms large shiny bubbles. Return linguine to large pot. Pour sauce over noodles; toss to thoroughly coat. Add Parmesan cheese; toss again.

5. Turn pasta into large bowl. Sprinkle with parsley.

4 to 6 servings.

Ginger's Springtime Noodles

UMM GOOD & HEALTHY LASAGNA

Cindy Blanton
York, South Carolina

1 tablespoon kosher (coarse) salt
1 (16-oz.) pkg. whole wheat lasagna
   noodles
1 lb. ground turkey breast
1 (15-oz.) can diced tomatoes
1 (15-oz.) container reduced-fat
   ricotta cheese
1 (10-oz.) pkg. frozen chopped
   spinach, thawed, squeezed dry
2 (8-oz.) cans tomato sauce
3 cups (12 oz.) shredded reduced-fat
   Italian cheese blend

1. Heat oven to 350°F. Spray 3-quart casserole with nonstick cooking spray.

2. Fill large pot two-thirds full of water; add 1 tablespoon salt. Bring to a boil over high heat. Cook lasagna noodles according to package directions; drain. Set aside.

3. In large skillet, cook turkey over medium-high heat until no longer pink in center. Stir in diced tomatoes and tomato sauce.

4. In small bowl, mix ricotta cheese and spinach. Spread small amount of turkey mixture over bottom of casserole. Add layer of noodles, 1/3 of the turkey mixture, 1/3 of the ricotta mixture and 1/3 of the cheese. Repeat twice. Bake 30 to 40 minutes or until heated through.

12 servings.

SAUSAGE AND PASTA DELIGHT

Tom Dello Stritto
Auburn, New York

1 lb. ground Italian sausage
1 1/2 tablespoons olive oil
1 large red bell pepper, diced
1 large yellow bell pepper, diced
1 medium onion, diced
4 to 5 zucchini, cut into bite-size
   pieces
5 to 6 garlic cloves, sliced
1 teaspoon dried oregano
1 teaspoon dried basil
1 teaspoon salt
1/8 freshly ground pepper
1 tablespoon chopped fresh parsley
1/4 cup marsala wine
1 (12-oz.) can reduced-sodium
   chicken broth
1 (8-oz.) pkg. rigatoni
3 tablespoons butter

1. In medium skillet, cook sausage over medium-high heat until no longer pink in center; drain excess fat.

2. In large skillet, heat oil over medium-high heat until hot. Sauté bell pepper, onion, zucchini, garlic, oregano, basil, salt, pepper and parsley until onion is transparent. Add wine, broth and sausage. Simmer 15 to 20 minutes or until mixture starts to glaze.

3. Meanwhile, fill large pot two-thirds full of water; add 1 tablespoon salt. Bring to a boil over high heat. Cook rigatoni according to package directions. Rinse and drain thoroughly.

4. Add pasta to skillet; stir well. Stir in butter. Sprinkle with freshly grated Parmesan cheese, if desired.

4 servings.

FETTUCCINE & ITALIAN RED SAUCE

Nikole Braue
Pontiac, Michigan

1 lb. ground beef or ground Italian
    sausage
2 tablespoons olive oil
1 large onion, diced
5 garlic cloves, minced
$1/2$ tablespoon Italian seasoning
1 (28-oz.) can chopped tomatoes
1 (28-oz.) can tomato puree
1 (15-oz.) can tomato paste
1 (28-oz.) can tomato sauce
1 (28-oz.) can water
1 cup red wine
$1 1/2$ teaspoons dried basil
$1 1/2$ teaspoons dried oregano
$1/2$ teaspoon cinnamon
$1/4$ teaspoon dried marjoram
2 tablespoons chopped fresh parsley
2 bay leaves
1 (16-oz.) pkg. fettuccine noodles

1. In large skillet, cook beef over medium-high heat until no longer pink in center; drain excess fat. Set aside.

2. In another large skillet, heat oil over medium-high heat until hot; sauté onion, garlic and Italian seasoning until onion is transparent. Add meat and chopped tomatoes; cook 2 minutes, stirring constantly.

3. Place mixture in slow cooker on high heat setting. Stir in tomato puree, tomato paste, tomato sauce, water, wine, basil, oregano, cinnamon, marjoram, parsley and bay leaves. Simmer at least 3 hours, stirring occasionally. Discard bay leaves.

4. Fill large pot two-thirds full of water; add 1 tablespoon salt. Bring to a boil over high heat. Cook fettuccine according to package directions; drain.

5. Place pasta in large bowl. Cover with tomato sauce. Sprinkle with freshly grated Parmesan cheese, if desired.

8 servings.

SPLENDID PASTA DISH

Susan Mazzoccoli
New Port Richey, Florida

$1/4$ cup olive oil
3 garlic cloves, sliced
1 medium eggplant, diced
1 red bell pepper, sliced
1 yellow bell pepper, sliced
1 orange bell pepper, sliced
1 zucchini, cut in half lengthwise,
    sliced into $1/4$-inch pieces
$1/8$ teaspoon salt
$1/4$ cup water
1 tablespoon kosher (coarse) salt
1 (8-oz.) pkg. penne, rigatoni or
    mostaccioli pasta

1. In large skillet, heat oil over medium-high heat until hot. Sauté garlic until light brown. Add eggplant, bell peppers and zucchini; sauté until soft. Season with $1/8$ teaspoon salt. Add water; cover and simmer until tender.

2. Fill large pot two-thirds full of water; add 1 tablespoon salt. Bring to a boil over high heat. Cook pasta according to package directions. Rinse and drain thoroughly in cool water.

3. Turn pasta into large bowl; cover with garlic sauce. Sprinkle with freshly grated Parmesan cheese, if desired.

4 servings.

Chicken in Ale

CHICKEN IN ALE

Kathy Goodman
Wichita, Kansas

1 tablespoon kosher (coarse) salt
1 (12-oz.) pkg. fettuccine
6 boneless skinless chicken breast
   halves (about 1¹/₂ lb.)
4 teaspoons vegetable oil
2 cups chopped onion
2¹/₂ cups chopped mixed fresh
   mushrooms (white, chanterelle,
   crimini, shiitake, etc.)
1¹/₄ cups reduced-sodium chicken
   broth
2 cups brown ale beer
4 teaspoons white wine or
   Worcestershire sauce
1 tablespoon snipped fresh thyme or
¹/₂ teaspoon dried
¹/₄ teaspoon salt
¹/₄ teaspoon freshly ground pepper
3 tablespoons all-purpose flour

1. Fill large pot two-thirds full of water; add 1 tablespoon salt. Bring to a boil over high heat. Cook fettuccine according to package directions; drain. Set aside.

2. Meanwhile, rinse chicken and pat dry. In large skillet, heat oil over medium-high heat until hot. Cook chicken and onion until chicken is brown. Add mushrooms, ³/₄ cup of the broth, ale, Worcestershire sauce, thyme, salt and pepper; bring to a boil and reduce heat. Cover and cook 5 minutes or until chicken is tender and juices run clear. Remove chicken breasts to serving platter; keep warm.

3. In screw-top jar, shake flour and remaining ¹/₂ cup broth. Add mixture to skillet. Cook, stirring constantly, until thickened and bubbly. Cook and stir an additional 1 minute. Serve chicken and sauce over fettuccine. Garnish with thyme sprigs.

6 servings.

COUNTRY STYLE RIBS AND PASTA

Georgia Nua
Palm Springs, California

2 lb. country-style pork ribs
1 teaspoon dried basil
¹/₂ teaspoon dried marjoram
¹/₂ teaspoon dried oregano
1 bay leaf
¹/₄ teaspoon dried thyme
¹/₈ teaspoon freshly ground pepper
2 garlic cloves, minced
1 tablespoon kosher (coarse) salt
4 oz. mostaccioli
¹/₂ tablespoon olive oil
6 large white mushrooms, sliced
1 onion, chopped
1 (28-oz.) jar spaghetti sauce

1. In large pot, combine ribs, basil, marjoram, oregano, bay leaf, thyme, pepper and garlic; cover with water. Boil over high heat 30 to 45 minutes or until meat pulls away from bone. If using boneless ribs, cook until no longer pink in center. Discard bay leaf.

2. Fill another large pot two-thirds full of water; add 1 tablespoon salt. Bring to a boil over high heat. Cook mostaccioli according to package directions. Rinse and drain thoroughly in cool water. Set aside.

3. In large skillet, heat oil over medium-high heat until hot. Sauté mushrooms and onion until onions are transparent. Remove from heat; add spaghetti sauce. Add cooked ribs to sauce mixture; turn to coat. Simmer and cook 20 to 30 minutes or until meat is very tender. Add pasta; stir to coat with sauce.

4 to 6 servings.

CHICKEN PASTA STIR-FRY

Rich Melcher
Yakima, Washington

4 (1-lb.) boneless, skinless chicken
    breast halves, cut into 1-inch
    pieces, marinated in Asian stir-fry
    sauce
4 to 5 drops sesame oil
2 teaspoons chili oil
$1/2$ teaspoon ground ginger
1 tablespoon kosher (coarse) salt
2 lb. spaghetti
1 (8-oz.) can sliced water chestnuts
3 garlic cloves, minced
$1/4$ cup chopped green bell pepper
$1/4$ cup chopped red bell pepper
$1/4$ cup chopped yellow bell pepper
6 to 8 Chinese pea pods, stem
    removed, sliced horizontally
6 baby corncobs, sliced
3 green onions, chopped
1 carrot, coarsely chopped
$1/8$ teaspoon Chinese five-spice powder
3 tablespoons safflower oil
$1/4$ cup low-sodium soy sauce
3 or 4 tablespoons Asian stir-fry or
    cooking sauce
$1/2$ cup dry-roasted peanuts or cashews

1. In wok, stir-fry chicken over medium-high heat in sesame oil, chili oil and ginger 4 to 6 minutes or until chicken is no longer pink in center; remove from wok.

2. Fill large pot two-thirds full of water; add 1 tablespoon salt. Bring to a boil over high heat. Cook spaghetti according to package directions. Rinse and drain spaghetti thoroughly in cool water. Set aside.

3. Meanwhile, stir-fry water chestnuts, garlic, bell peppers, pea pods, corncobs, green onions and carrot. Remove vegetables from wok and place in separate bowl.

4. Add safflower oil to wok; stir-fry pasta 4 to 5 minutes. Stir in chicken and vegetables; heat thoroughly. Add soy sauce, stir-fry sauce and nuts. Stir-fry an additional 1 minute.

4 servings.

CHICKEN VEGETABLE LINGUINE

Carole Anne Barbaro
Clayton, New Jersey

1 tablespoon kosher (coarse) salt
1 (8-oz.) pkg. linguine
$1/4$ cup vegetable oil
3 large garlic cloves, sliced
2 (1-lb.) boneless skinless chicken
    breast halves, cut into 1-inch pieces
1 medium onion, chopped
$1/4$ cup olive oil
1 medium zucchini, sliced
1 medium yellow squash, sliced
1 tomato, chopped
1 (14-oz.) can reduced-sodium
    chicken broth
3 fresh mushrooms
$1/2$ cup chopped fresh spinach
2 tablespoons butter

1. Fill large pot two-thirds full of water; add 1 tablespoon salt. Bring to a boil over high heat. Cook linguine according to package directions. Rinse and drain linguine thoroughly in cool water. Set aside.

2. Meanwhile, in large skillet, heat oil over medium-high heat until hot. Sauté garlic, chicken and onion 5 minutes or until onion is transparent. Reduce heat to low. Stir in olive oil, zucchini and squash. Cook, covered, 5 minutes, stirring occasionally. Add tomato, broth, mushrooms, spinach and butter; toss gently.

3. Pour vegetables over pasta; toss gently. Sprinkle with freshly grated Parmesan cheese, if desired.

4 servings.

LIGHT MEATLESS PASTITSIO

Naomi Golovin
Cleveland, Ohio

1 tablespoon olive oil
1 onion, chopped
1 garlic clove, minced
2 (15-oz.) cans pinto beans, drained
1 (16-oz.) can tomato sauce
$1/2$ cup dry red wine
1 small bay leaf
$1/4$ cup chopped fresh parsley
$1/2$ teaspoon cinnamon
$1/2$ teaspoon dried basil
1 teaspoon dried oregano
$1/4$ teaspoon salt
$1/4$ teaspoon freshly ground pepper
2 tablespoons butter
$4^1/2$ cups milk
$3/4$ cup all-purpose flour
Dash nutmeg
2 eggs
1 cup (4 oz.) ricotta cheese
1 tablespoon kosher (coarse) salt
1 (12-oz.) pkg. ziti
$3/4$ (3 oz.) cup freshly grated
   Parmesan cheese

1. Heat oven to 400°F. Spray 13x9-inch pan with nonstick cooking spray.

2. In large skillet, heat oil over medium-high heat until hot. Sauté onion and garlic until onion is transparent. Add beans and partially mash them. Stir in tomato sauce, wine, bay leaf, parsley, cinnamon, basil, oregano, $1/8$ teaspoon salt and $1/8$ teaspoon freshly ground pepper; simmer about 30 minutes or until most of the liquid has been absorbed. Discard bay leaf.

3. In small saucepan, melt butter over medium heat. In large bowl, combine 4 cups of the milk and flour; whisk into saucepan. Reduce heat to low; stir about 15 minutes or until thickened. Season with $1/8$ teaspoon salt, $1/8$ teaspoon pepper and nutmeg.

4. Mix remaining $1/2$ cup milk with eggs. Stir 1 cup of the warm milk mixture into eggs, then return to cream sauce. Beat in ricotta.

5. Fill large pot two-thirds full of water; add 1 tablespoon salt. Bring to a boil over high heat. Cook ziti according to package directions. Rinse and drain ziti thoroughly in cool water. Set aside.

6. Spread half of the pasta evenly in pan. Sprinkle with half of the Parmesan cheese. Pour half the cream sauce over the Parmesan cheese. Spread bean sauce evenly over cream sauce. Spread with remaining pasta and cream sauce. Top with grated cheese.

7. Bake 1 hour or until golden brown.

6 servings.

A DIFFERENT KIND OF LASAGNA

Debby Pfeiffer
Canyon Lake, Texas

1 teaspoon olive oil
1/2 lb. ground beef
1 1/2 cups chopped onions
1 (14-oz.) can pinto beans
1 tablespoon diced jalapeño chile
1 garlic clove, minced
1 (4-oz.) can diced green chiles
4 cups tomato sauce
2 teaspoons chili powder
1 teaspoon Italian seasoning
1 cup white wine or water
1 (8-oz.) container cottage cheese
1 1/2 cups (6 oz.) shredded mozzarella, Monterey Jack or colby cheese
1 egg
16 oz. lasagna noodles

1. Heat oven to 350°F. Spray 13x9-inch pan with nonstick cooking spray.

2. In large skillet, heat oil over medium-high heat until hot. Cook beef and onions until onions are transparent. Stir in beans, jalapeños, garlic, chiles, tomato sauce, chili powder, Italian seasoning and wine. Simmer 20 minutes.

3. In medium bowl, combine cottage cheese, shredded cheese and egg; mix well. Set aside.

4. Pour 3/4 cup of the meat sauce in bottom of pan. Layer noodles and cheese mixture. Continue until meat and cheese mixtures are gone, with cheese layer on top.

5. Cover with aluminum foil and bake 30 minutes. Remove foil and bake an additional 15 minutes.

4 servings.

NOTE Omit jalapeño, chili powder and green chiles and change mozzarella cheese to Romano, Swiss or Parmesan to make regular lasagna. Or try using spinach added to regular lasagna.

MEDITERRANEAN FETTUCCINE SALAD

Danielle Balint
Long Beach, California

1 tablespoon kosher (coarse) salt
1 (9-oz.) pkg. fresh herbed fettuccine
1 bunch chopped fresh cilantro
1 (4-oz.) container crumbled garlic feta cheese
1 (8- to 12-oz.) jar sun-dried tomatoes, coarsely chopped
1/8 teaspoon salt
1/8 teaspoon freshly ground pepper

1. Fill large pot two-thirds full of water; add 1 tablespoon salt. Bring to a boil over high heat. Cook fettuccine according to package directions. Rinse and drain fettuccine thoroughly in cool water. Set aside.

2. In large bowl, combine cilantro, cheese, tomatoes, salt and pepper; mix well. Add fettuccine; toss gently. Refrigerate at least 30 minutes before serving.

3 to 4 servings.

Mediterranean Fettuccine Salad

CREAMY CAJUN CHICKEN AND PASTA

Kelly King
Bismarck, North Dakota

4 (1-lb.) boneless skinless chicken
  breast halves, cut into 1-inch strips
5 teaspoons Cajun seasoning
1/4 cup butter
1 green bell pepper, cut into
  1-inch strips
1 red bell pepper, cut into
  1-inch strips
2 (8-oz.) jars whole mushrooms,
  halved
8 green onions, sliced
1 cup heavy cream
1/4 teaspoon dried basil
1/4 teaspoon lemon pepper
1/4 teaspoon salt
1/8 teaspoon garlic powder
1/8 teaspoon freshly ground pepper
1 tablespoon kosher (coarse) salt
1 lb. linguine

1. In large resealable plastic bag, combine chicken and Cajun seasoning; shake to coat.

2. In large skillet, melt butter over medium-high heat. Sauté seasoned chicken 7 minutes or until chicken is no longer pink in center. Add bell peppers, mushrooms and onion; cook and stir 7 minutes or until peppers are soft. Add cream, basil, lemon pepper, 1/4 teaspoon salt, garlic powder and pepper; mix well and heat through.

3. Fill large pot two-thirds full of water; add 1 tablespoon salt. Bring to a boil over high heat. Cook linguine according to package directions; drain.

4. Add linguine to chicken mixture; toss to coat. Sprinkle with freshly grated Parmesan cheese, if desired.

6 servings.

SHRIMP WITH VEGETABLES OVER ANGEL HAIR

Lisa Thompson
Westfield, Massachusetts

1 tablespoon butter
1 large garlic clove, minced
1/4 cup scallions, chopped
1/4 cup white wine
1 tablespoon fresh lemon juice
1 zucchini, sliced
1 yellow squash, sliced
1 tablespoon kosher (coarse) salt
8 oz. angel hair pasta
1/2 lb. shelled deveined medium
  shrimp
2 plum tomatoes, diced

1. In large skillet, melt butter over medium-high heat. Sauté garlic and scallions; add wine and lemon juice. Set aside and keep warm.

2. Steam zucchini and squash. Set aside and keep warm.

3. Meanwhile, fill large pot two-thirds full of water; add 1 tablespoon salt. Bring to a boil over high heat. Cook angel hair according to package directions.

4. Place shrimp in colander. Drain pasta over shrimp to heat.

5. To serve, pour sauce over shrimp and pasta; top with tomatoes, zucchini and squash.

2 servings.

ITALIAN STEAK AND PASTA

Jennifer A. Smindak
Johnstown, Pennsylvania

2 tablespoons olive oil
1 lb. top round steak (1/2 inch thick)
1 medium onion, sliced
1 red bell pepper, sliced
1 green bell pepper, sliced
3 garlic cloves, minced
1 (8-oz.) pkg. fresh mushrooms, sliced
1 medium zucchini, sliced
1 tablespoon kosher (coarse) salt
1 (16-oz.) pkg. farfalle (bow-tie pasta)
1 (14.5-oz.) can diced tomatoes
1 (6-oz.) can tomato paste
1 cup water
1 teaspoon salt
1/4 teaspoon freshly ground pepper
1 teaspoon dried oregano
1 teaspoon dried basil
1/2 teaspoon crushed red pepper
1/4 teaspoon dried thyme

1. In large skillet, heat 1 tablespoon of the oil over medium-high heat until hot. Cook steak until brown on both sides. Remove steak from skillet; set aside and keep warm.

2. Add remaining tablespoon oil to skillet; sauté onions, bell peppers and garlic until vegetables are partially softened. Add mushrooms and zucchini; sauté until soft.

3. Meanwhile, fill large pot two-thirds full of water; add 1 tablespoon salt. Bring to a boil over high heat. Cook farfalle according to package directions. Rinse and drain farfalle thoroughly in cool water. Set aside.

4. Add tomatoes, tomato paste, water, salt, pepper, oregano, basil, parsley, red pepper and thyme to vegetable mixture. Cover and simmer over medium heat about 15 to 20 minutes or until mixture thickens.

5. Slice steak into 1-inch-thick strips; add to tomato mixture. Cook an additional 20 minutes. Add pasta to tomato mixture; cook until heated through. Sprinkle with freshly grated Parmesan cheese, if desired.

6 servings.

SHRIMP LINGUINE IN GARLIC SAUCE

Vivian Nikanow
Chicago, Illinois

1/4 cup butter
1 lb. shelled, deveined uncooked medium shrimp
4 to 5 garlic cloves, minced
1/4 cup chopped fresh Italian parsley
2 cups heavy cream
1 tablespoon kosher (coarse) salt
1/4 teaspoon salt
1/8 teaspoon freshly ground pepper
1 (16-oz.) pkg. linguine

1. In large skillet, melt butter over medium-high heat. Sauté shrimp until tender. Remove shrimp from pan; set aside. Add garlic to skillet; sauté until golden brown.

2. Stir in parsley and cream; boil about 5 minutes or until reduced by half, stirring frequently. Season with 1/8 teaspoon salt and pepper. Add shrimp to garlic sauce.

3. Fill large pot two-thirds full of water; add 1 tablespoon salt. Bring to a boil over high heat. Cook linguine according to package directions. Rinse and drain linguine thoroughly in cool water. Transfer to large bowl.

4. Pour garlic sauce over linguine. Sprinkle with freshly grated Parmesan cheese, if desired.

4 servings.

Italian Ravioli

ITALIAN RAVIOLI

Marie Pennington
Rio Rancho, New Mexico

DOUGH
4 cups all-purpose flour
4 large eggs
2 tablespoons vegetable oil
3/4 cup warm water
1 tablespoon kosher (coarse) salt

FILLING
2 cups finely chopped cooked beef
  roast
2 cups finely chopped cooked pork
  roast
1/4 teaspoon salt
1/4 teaspoon freshly ground pepper
1 tablespoon chopped fresh oregano
1 tablespoon chopped fresh rosemary
1 tablespoon chopped fresh basil
2 tablespoons freshly grated Parmesan
  cheese
1 garlic clove, minced
1/2 cup finely chopped cooked spinach
3 eggs

SAUCE
2 tablespoons olive oil
1 large onion, chopped
1 garlic clove, minced
2 (6-oz.) cans tomato paste
4 cups water
1/4 teaspoon salt
1/2 teaspoon freshly ground pepper
1/4 cup chopped fresh oregano
1/4 cup chopped fresh rosemary
1/4 cup chopped fresh basil

1. In large bowl, make well in middle of flour; add 4 eggs, oil and water. Gather dough; knead on lightly-floured surface about 10 minutes or until soft and elastic. Cover dough with clean kitchen towel. Let rest 30 minutes.

2. Meanwhile, to make filling, combine beef and pork roasts. Season with salt, pepper, oregano, rosemary and basil; mix well. Add garlic, spinach and 3 eggs; mix well. Set aside.

3. To make sauce, heat oil over medium-high heat until hot. Sauté onion and garlic until onion is transparent. Add tomato paste and water alternately, stirring constantly. Add salt, pepper, oregano, rosemary and basil; let simmer, partially covered, over low heat 1 hour.

4. Meanwhile, divide dough into thirds. Roll each piece into rectangle 30x11 inches. (Keep remaining dough covered when rolling out each piece.) Place teaspoonfuls of meat filling on side of dough rectangle about 2 inches apart. Fold other half of dough over filling. Cut along row with ravioli cutter, pastry wheel or knife. Press edges with fork dipped in flour to form square mounds of ravioli.

5. Fill large pot two-thirds full of water; add 1 tablespoon salt. Bring to a boil over high heat. Cook ravioli according to package directions; drain. Transfer to large bowl. Pour sauce over ravioli. Sprinkle with freshly grated Parmesan cheese, if desired.

6 servings.

NOTE To freeze, place uncooked ravioli on flour-dusted cookie sheet and put in freezer until ravioli are frozen. Transfer them to freezer bags and keep up to 4 months. Cook in boiling water while still frozen.

ANGEL HAIR PASTA WITH CHICKEN

Tammy Raynes
Natchitoches, Louisiana

2 tablespoons olive oil
2 (about $^1/_2$ lb.) boneless skinless
   chicken breast halves, cut into
   1-inch pieces
1 carrot, sliced diagonally into
   $^1/_4$-inch pieces
1 (10-oz.) pkg. frozen broccoli
   florets, thawed
2 garlic cloves, minced
$^2/_3$ cup reduced-sodium chicken broth
1 teaspoon dried basil
2 tablespoons freshly grated Parmesan
   cheese
1 tablespoon kosher (coarse) salt
1 (12-oz.) pkg. angel hair pasta

1. In large skillet, heat 1 tablespoon of the oil over medium heat until hot; cook chicken 5 minutes or until no longer pink in center, stirring occasionally. Remove chicken from skillet; drain on paper towels.

2. Heat remaining 1 tablespoon oil over medium-high heat in same skillet until hot. Sauté carrots, broccoli and garlic until tender. Add broth, basil and cheese; stir to combine. Return chicken to skillet; toss gently. Reduce heat and simmer 4 minutes.

3. Fill large pot two-thirds full of water; add 1 tablespoon salt. Bring to a boil over high heat. Cook angel hair according to package directions; drain.

4. In large bowl, pour chicken and vegetable mixture over pasta. Sprinkle with additional freshly grated Parmesan cheese, if desired.

4 servings.

HAM LASAGNA WITH BASIL

Kathy Hickey
Ashley, Pennsylvania

PASTA
1 tablespoon kosher (coarse) salt
1 (8-oz.) pkg. lasagna noodles

BASIL SAUCE
2 garlic cloves, minced
1 cup (4 oz.) freshly grated Parmesan
   cheese
2 tablespoons olive oil
2 cups chopped fresh basil

WHITE SAUCE
$1^1/_2$ tablespoons butter
3 tablespoons all-purpose flour
$^1/_2$ teaspoon salt
$^1/_8$ teaspoon cayenne pepper
$^1/_8$ teaspoon nutmeg
$1^1/_2$ cups milk
$^1/_2$ lb. thinly sliced ham
1 cup (4 oz.) shredded cheddar
   cheese

1. Heat oven to 325°F. Spray 8-inch square pan with nonstick cooking spray.

2. Fill large pot two-thirds full of water; add 1 tablespoon salt. Bring to a boil over high heat. Cook lasagna noodles according to package directions; drain. Set aside.

3. For basil sauce, puree garlic, cheese, oil and basil in food processor. For white sauce, melt butter in small skillet; stir in flour. Cook over low heat 3 minutes; stir in cayenne and nutmeg. Slowly add milk; cook until thickened.

4. Spoon $^1/_4$ cup of the sauce in bottom of pan. Alternately layer noodles, one-third of the ham, one-third of the basil sauce, one-fourth of the white sauce and one-fourth of the cheese. Repeat second and third layers. For final layer, top noodles with remaining white sauce and cheese. Bake 25 minutes.

4 servings.

MEAT MAIN DISHES

BEEF BURGUNDY

David A. Heppner
Brandon, Florida

1 (2½-lb.) lean boneless round steak,
  cut into 1-inch cubes
4 garlic cloves, minced
2 cups dry red wine
1 (10¾-oz.) can condensed cream of
  mushroom soup
1 (10.5-oz.) can consommé
1 (1-oz.) pkg. onion soup mix
6 cups sliced fresh mushrooms
1 (16-oz.) pkg. frozen pearl onions
3 tablespoons all-purpose flour
½ cup water
2 (12-oz.) pkg. medium egg noodles
¼ cup (1 oz.) freshly grated
  Parmesan cheese
¾ cup sour cream

1. Heat oven to 350°F. Spray Dutch oven with non-stick cooking spray.

2. Heat Dutch oven over medium-high heat until hot. Cook steak 9 minutes or until no longer pink in center. Drain well; set aside.

3. Spray Dutch oven with cooking spray again; place over medium heat. Sauté garlic 1 minute. Add wine, soup, consommé and onion soup mix; stir well and bring to a boil. Return steak to Dutch oven; stir in mushrooms and onions. Remove from heat.

4. In small bowl, whisk flour and water; add to steak mixture, stirring well. Cover and bake 1 hours.

5. Cook noodles according to package directions; drain well. Transfer noodles to large serving bowl. Add cheese and sour cream; toss gently to coat. Serve steak mixture over noodles.

6 to 8 servings.

CHILI-CHEESE STEAK

Vera Jacobs
Chico, California

1 cup all-purpose flour
1 teaspoon garlic powder
1 teaspoon fines herbes
1 teaspoon salt
1½ teaspoons carne asada mix*
4 steaks (1 inch thick)
3 tablespoons olive oil
2 (7-oz.) cans diced green chiles
3 fresh tomatoes, coarsely chopped
2 cups (8 oz.) shredded cheddar
  cheese

1. In 3-quart casserole, combine flour, garlic powder, fines herbes, salt and carne asada; mix well. Dredge steaks in mixture.

2. In large skillet, heat oil over medium-high heat until hot. Cook steak until brown on both sides. Reduce heat to medium-low. Spread chopped chiles over meat and surface of pan; cover and cook until meat is tender. Spread tomatoes over layer of chiles; cook until tomatoes are just hot and juicy. Just before serving, sprinkle with cheese. Cover and cook just until cheese is melted.

4 servings.

TIP *If you do not have carne asada seasoning, substitute equal parts cumin, black pepper, oregano, cayenne pepper and chili powder.

DIJON-WINE MARINATED ROSEMARY ROAST

Kathy Hickey
Ashley, Pennsylvania

1 (3- to 4-lb.) boneless rib-eye roast
   or rump roast
$1/_2$ cup red wine
1 tablespoon freshly ground pepper
2 tablespoons olive oil
1 tablespoon Dijon mustard
$1/_2$ teaspoon salt
1 teaspoon fresh rosemary or
   $1/_2$ teaspoon dried
1 garlic clove, crushed

1. Place roast in large resealable plastic bag.

2. In medium bowl, combine wine, pepper, oil, mustard, salt, rosemary and garlic; mix well. Pour marinade over roast. Seal bag; refrigerate 8 hours.

3. Heat oven to 350°F. Remove roast from marinade; discard marinade.

4. Place roast in 3-quart casserole. Bake 1$3/_4$ hours or until internal temperature reaches at least 160°F.

10 to 12 servings.

MARINATED FLANK STEAK WITH LEMON-HERB BUTTER

Kathy Hickey
Ashley, Pennsylvania

STEAK
1 (1- to 1$1/_2$-lb.) flank steak
$1/_4$ cup vegetable oil
$1/_4$ cup dry red wine
2 teaspoons dry mustard
2 teaspoons low-sodium soy sauce
1 tablespoon Worcestershire sauce
1 garlic clove, minced
$1/_2$ teaspoon salt
$1/_4$ teaspoon sugar

LEMON-HERB BUTTER
$1/_3$ cup butter, softened
1$1/_2$ tablespoons fresh lemon juice
3 tablespoons chopped fresh parsley
3 tablespoons watercress, stems
   removed
1 teaspoon Worcestershire sauce
$1/_4$ teaspoon tarragon
Dash ground white pepper

1. Place steak in large resealable plastic bag. In blender, combine oil, wine, mustard, soy sauce, Worcestershire sauce, garlic, salt and sugar; mix well. Pour marinade over steak. Seal bag; refrigerate up to 8 hours in refrigerator, turning once or twice. Remove steak from marinade; reserve marinade. Heat marinade to a boil over high heat in medium saucepan. Set aside and keep warm.

2. Heat broiler. Broil steak 4 to 6 inches from heat until no longer pink in center, brushing occasionally with marinade and turning once.

3. To make Lemon-Herb Butter, beat butter at medium speed until fluffy. Gradually beat in lemon juice, parsley, watercress, Worcestershire sauce, tarragon and white pepper. Shape in to log; refrigerate until ready to use. Slice steak thinly. Serve topped with thin slices of Lemon-Herb Butter.

4 to 6 servings.

DRESSED UP HAM STEAK

Christina Freeman
Pascagoula, Mississippi

1 (2-lb.) ham steak, cut from center
  of ham ($^1/_2$ inch thick)
2 tablespoons packed brown sugar
1 teaspoon horseradish mustard
1 teaspoon fresh pineapple juice
2 (8-oz.) cans sliced pineapple,
  drained

1. In large skillet over medium heat, lightly brown ham steak on one side.

2. In small bowl, combine brown sugar, mustard and pineapple juice; mix well. Spread over top of steak; top with pineapple slices. Cook 5 minutes. Turn pineapple slices over. Serve hot.

6 servings.

STEAK CARAWAY

Elaine Weisheit
Quincy, Illinois

1 tablespoon vegetable oil
4 (1-lb.) cube steaks
3 tablespoons packed brown sugar
1 tablespoon vinegar
2 tablespoons caraway seed
1 (.87-oz.) pkg. brown gravy mix
1 cup water
1 (4-oz.) can sliced mushrooms,
  drained

1. In large skillet, heat oil over medium-high heat until hot. Cook steaks until no longer pink in center and juices run clear. Remove steaks from pan and keep warm. Stir in brown sugar, vinegar, caraway seeds and gravy mix. Stir in 1 cup water; whisk until smooth. Stir mixture into skillet.

2. Cover and simmer until sauce thickens. Stir in mushrooms. Serve steaks with gravy, boiled potatoes and cabbage, if desired.

4 servings.

TARRAGON VEAL ROLLS

Kathy Hickey
Ashley, Pennsylvania

2 lb. veal cutlets
$^1/_4$ cup all-purpose flour
1 tablespoon butter
$^1/_4$ cup chopped celery
$^1/_4$ cup chopped green onion
2 cups dry bread crumbs
1 egg
$1^1/_4$ teaspoons tarragon, divided
1 teaspoon minced lemon peel
1 tablespoon olive oil
$^1/_4$ cup fresh orange or lemon juice
$^1/_4$ cup reduced-sodium chicken broth

1. Sprinkle each cutlet with flour; shake off excess.

2. In large skillet, melt butter over medium heat. Sauté celery and onions until onions are transparent. Stir in bread crumbs, egg, 1 teaspoon of the tarragon and lemon peel; combine well. Spoon stuffing onto each cutlet. Roll up; secure with toothpicks.

3. In another large skillet, heat oil over medium-high heat until hot. Brown veal on both sides. Add remaining $^1/_4$ teaspoon tarragon, juice and wine to skillet. Cover and simmer 25 minutes; add water if needed. Remove toothpicks. Place veal on platter. Spoon juices over veal. Garnish with lemon slices.

6 to 8 servings.

Tarragon Veal Rolls

NAPOLEAN STEAK

Walleen Hopkins
Sandy, Oregon

1 (2-lb.) round steak (1 inch thick)
2 tablespoons all-purpose flour
2 tablespoons vegetable oil
1 cup diced onion
$1/2$ cup diced celery
2 garlic cloves, minced
1 teaspoon salt
$1/2$ teaspoon freshly ground pepper
$1/2$ cup reduced-sodium beef broth
1 bay leaf
$1/4$ teaspoon oregano
2 (8-oz.) cans tomato sauce
$1/2$ cup red wine
1 cup sliced mushrooms

1. Heat oven to 350°F. Spray 3-quart casserole with nonstick cooking spray.

2. Pound flour into both sides of steak; cut into serving pieces.

3. In large skillet, heat oil over medium-high heat until hot. Cook steak until brown on both sides. Remove steak from skillet; set aside. Lightly brown onion, celery and garlic. Return steak to skillet; heat thoroughly. Season with salt and pepper.

4. Place mixture in casserole; add broth, bay leaf, oregano, tomato sauce, wine and mushrooms. Cover and bake $1^1/2$ hours or until beef is tender. Discard bay leaf.

4 to 6 servings.

SUMMER-STUFFED PEPPERS

Tammy Raynes
Natchitoches, Louisiana

8 medium green bell peppers
$1^1/2$ lb. ground beef
1 onion, finely chopped
1 carrot, shredded
$1/2$ cup finely chopped cabbage
$1/2$ cup shredded zucchini
1 garlic clove, minced
1 (28-oz.) can diced tomatoes
$1/2$ cup long-grain rice
1 tablespoon packed brown sugar
$1/4$ teaspoon dried basil
$1/8$ teaspoon freshly ground pepper

1. Cut tops off each bell pepper and set aside. Remove seeds and membranes.

2. In medium pot, cook bell peppers and tops in boiling water 2 to 3 minutes or until crisp-tender. Remove and drain on paper towels. Remove stems from pepper tops; chop enough of the tops to make $1/3$ cup. Set aside.

3. In large skillet, cook beef over medium heat until brown. Sauté onion, carrot, cabbage, zucchini, garlic and chopped bell pepper until tender. Add tomatoes, rice, brown sugar, basil and pepper. Reduce heat; cover and simmer 20 minutes or until rice is tender. Stuff hot meat mixture into bell peppers.

8 servings.

PORK, CASHEW AND GREEN BEAN STIR-FRY

David A. Heppner
Brandon, Florida

$1/4$ cup low-sodium soy sauce
2 teaspoons cornstarch
1 (1-lb.) pork tenderloin, cut
   into $1/4$-inch slices
4 cups sliced green beans
   (2 inch thick)
2 teaspoons dark sesame oil
2 tablespoons minced fresh ginger
2 garlic cloves, minced
$1/4$ cup reduced-sodium chicken broth
2 cups hot cooked rice
$1/4$ cup chopped unsalted cashews,
   toasted

1. In medium bowl, combine soy sauce and cornstarch; mix well. Add pork; stir to coat. Cover and refrigerate.

2. Meanwhile, in large saucepan, cook beans in boiling water 5 minutes; drain and plunge into ice water. Drain again.

3. In large skillet, heat oil over medium-high heat until hot. Sauté ginger and garlic 1 minute. Stir-fry pork mixture $1^{1}/_{2}$ minutes. Stir in beans; stir-fry $1^{1}/_{2}$ minutes. Cook until pork is no longer pink in center. Stir in broth; reduce heat and simmer 2 minutes. Serve over rice and sprinkle with cashews.

4 servings.

PEAR-STUFFED TENDERLOIN

David A. Heppner
Brandon, Florida

1 cup chopped ripe pears
$1/4$ cup almonds, toasted
$1/4$ cup fresh bread crumbs
$1/4$ cup finely shredded carrot
2 tablespoons chopped onion
$1/8$ teaspoon ground ginger
$1/4$ teaspoon salt
$1/4$ teaspoon freshly ground pepper
1 (1-lb.) pork tenderloin
2 tablespoons orange marmalade

1. Heat oven to 425°F.

2. In medium bowl, combine pears, almonds, bread crumbs, carrot, onion, ginger, salt and pepper; mix well. Set side.

3. Make lengthwise cut three-fourths through tenderloin; open and flatten to $1/4$ inch thickness. Spread pear mixture over tenderloin. Roll up from long side; tuck in ends. Secure with toothpicks. Place tenderloin on rack in shallow roasting pan. Brush lightly with marinade.

4. Bake 20 to 25 minutes or until internal temperature reaches 160°F. Let stand 5 minutes; discard toothpicks.

3 to 4 servings.

Pork Tenderloin with Maple Barbecue Sauce

PORK TENDERLOIN WITH MAPLE BARBECUE SAUCE

Harold Demars
Rockford, Illinois

1 (1-lb.) pork tenderloin
$^1/_3$ cup pure maple syrup
$^1/_4$ cup honey
2 tablespoons barbecue sauce
1 tablespoon Dijon mustard

1. Place pork in large resealable plastic bag.

2. In small bowl, combine syrup, honey, barbecue sauce and mustard; mix well. Cover pork with marinade. Seal bag; refrigerate at least 2 hours. Remove pork from marinade; discard marinade.

3. Heat oven to 425°F. Spray 3-quart casserole with nonstick cooking spray. Place pork in casserole. Bake 20 to 25 minutes or until internal temperature reaches 160°F. Let stand 5 minutes before slicing.

4 servings.

THAI PORK MAIN DISH SALAD

Laurene H. Emerson
Yankeetown, Florida

1 tablespoon vegetable oil
1 lb. ground pork
1 large onion, chopped
2 tablespoons grated fresh ginger
3 cups hot cooked rice
$^1/_2$ cup dry roasted peanuts
$^1/_2$ cup chopped fresh cilantro
$^1/_8$ teaspoon crushed red pepper
$^1/_2$ teaspoon salt
$^1/_4$ cup fresh lime juice

1. In large skillet, heat oil over medium-high heat until hot. Sauté pork and onion with ginger over medium heat until pork is no longer pink in center. Remove from heat.

2. In large bowl, combine onion, rice, peanuts, cilantro, red pepper, salt and lime juice to skillet; mix well. Pour mixture into serving bowl; toss well.

4 servings.

HAM AND ASPARAGUS AU GRATIN

David A. Heppner–Brandon, Florida

6 slices baked ham
24 asparagus spears, cooked, drained
2 large eggs
2 egg yolks
$1^1/_2$ cups heavy cream
$^1/_8$ teaspoon salt
$^1/_8$ teaspoon freshly ground pepper
2 tablespoons shredded Swiss cheese
2 tablespoons freshly grated Parmesan cheese
1 tablespoon fresh parsley

1. Heat oven to 350°F. Spray 11x7-inch pan with nonstick cooking spray.

2. Wrap each ham slice around 4 asparagus spears; place seam side down in pan. In medium bowl, beat together eggs, yolks, cream, salt and pepper at medium speed until frothy. Pour mixture over ham rolls.

3. Bake 35 minutes or until top begins to brown and knife inserted into mixture comes out clean. Sprinkle with cheeses and parsley. Serve immediately.

6 servings.

STUFFED ZUCCHINI

Carole Anne Barbaro
Clayton, New Jersey

1 tablespoon kosher (coarse) salt
3 medium zucchini
1 lb. Italian sausage
$1/2$ cup seasoned bread crumbs
1 egg, beaten
$1/4$ cup (1-oz.) freshly grated
    Parmesan cheese

1. Heat oven to 375°F. Spray 3-quart casserole with nonstick cooking spray.

2. Cut zucchini in half lengthwise. Fill large pot two-thirds full of water; add 1 tablespoon salt. Bring to a boil over high heat. Cook zucchini until just tender. Remove zucchini; scrape pulp into colander to drain. Remove sausage from casing. In large skillet, cook sausage over medium heat until no longer pink in center. In large bowl, combine drained pulp, sausage, bread crumbs and egg; mix gently.

3. Fill cooked zucchini shells with mixture. Sprinkle with cheese. Place in casserole; bake 20 minutes or until golden brown.

6 servings.

AUTUMN PORK CHOPS

Jennifer Okutman
Westminster, Maryland

2 tablespoons vegetable oil
4 boneless pork chops
2 tablespoons butter
2 to 3 Granny Smith apples, sliced
$1/2$ cup apple jelly
$1/2$ teaspoon cinnamon
$1/4$ teaspoon nutmeg
3 tablespoons cranberry juice
$1/2$ cup coarsely chopped walnuts or
    pecans

1. In large skillet, heat oil over medium-high heat until hot. Cook pork until brown on both sides and slightly pink in center. Remove from heat; set aside.

2. In same skillet, melt butter over medium heat. Cook apples, jelly, cinnamon, nutmeg and juice until apples are slightly softened. Return pork chops to skillet; stir in nuts just before serving.

4 servings.

BEST EVER MEATBALLS

Bonnie Bewsey–Beecher, Illinois

2 lb. ground beef
1 medium onion, chopped
$1/8$ teaspoon salt
$1/8$ teaspoon freshly ground pepper
1 cup old-fashioned or quick-cooking
    oats
$1/2$ cup milk
2 cups ketchup
1 cup packed brown sugar
2 tablespoons mustard
2 tablespoons Worcestershire sauce

1. Heat oven to 350°F. Spray 13x9-inch pan with nonstick cooking spray.

2. In large bowl, combine beef, onion, salt, pepper, oats and milk; mix well. Shape mixture into 12 ($1\frac{1}{2}$-inch) meatballs. Place in pan.

3. In medium bowl, combine ketchup, brown sugar, mustard and Worcestershire sauce. Pour mixture over meatballs. Bake 1 hour or until internal temperature reaches 160°F.

6 to 8 servings.

Autumn Pork Chops

EGGPLANT SALTIMBOCA

Dave Bolick—Aurora, Colorado

SALTIMBOCA

$1/2$ cup vegetable oil
2 large eggplants, peeled, sliced into
    $1/4$-inch rounds
$3/4$ cup milk
1 tablespoon olive oil
2 garlic cloves, minced
1 (10-oz.) pkg. frozen baby spinach,
    thawed
$1/8$ teaspoon salt
$1/8$ teaspoon freshly ground pepper
2 eggs
$1/2$ cup all-purpose flour
1 cup dry bread crumbs

NEOPOLITAN SAUCE

$1/4$ cup olive oil
1 onion, chopped
$1/2$ cup dry white wine
1 (28-oz.) can diced Italian tomatoes
2 tablespoons capers
2 garlic cloves, minced
$1/2$ cup chopped ripe olives
$1/8$ teaspoon salt
$1/8$ teaspoon freshly ground pepper
2 tablespoons chopped fresh parsley
$1/2$ lb. sliced provolone cheese
4 to 6 oz. prosciutto, thinly sliced
1 bunch fresh basil
$1/4$ cup (1-oz.) freshly grated
    Parmigiano-Reggiano cheese

1. Heat oven to 450°F.

2. In 3-quart casserole, soak eggplant slices in milk.

3. In large skillet, heat $1/4$ cup of the olive oil over medium heat until hot; cook garlic 1 minute, stirring constantly, until fragrant. Add spinach, salt and pepper; sauté 2 minutes. Spoon spinach mixture into large bowl. Whisk eggs into small bowl until mixed. Remove eggplant from milk; drain on paper towels. Lightly dust eggplant with flour. Dip eggplant into egg wash, then into bread crumbs.

4. Heat remaining $1/4$ cup olive oil over medium-high heat. Fry eggplant in oil, 3 or 4 pieces at a time, 30 seconds per side or until lightly browned.

5. To make Neopolitan Sauce, heat oil over medium heat until hot; sauté onion 10 to 12 minutes or until onion releases juices. Add wine; increase heat to medium-high. Cook 2 to 3 minutes. Stir in tomatoes; cook 20 minutes. Add capers, garlic and olives; simmer 3 minutes. Add salt, pepper and parsley; remove from heat.

6. Place layer of fried eggplant into casserole. Top with layer of provolone, prosciutto, spinach mixture, basil and Neopolitan Sauce. Repeat with two additional layers. Top with sauce and grated cheese. Bake 15 to 20 minutes or until cheese is melted.

8 servings.

CHICKEN FRIED ROUND STEAK

Tammy Raynes—Natchitoches, Louisiana

2 lb. top round steak ($1/2$ inch thick)
2 eggs, beaten
2 tablespoons milk
2 cups crushed butter crackers
$1/4$ cup vegetable oil
$1/4$ teaspoon salt
$1/8$ teaspoon freshly ground pepper

1. Pound steak with meat mallet until $1/4$ inch thick; cut into 1-inch pieces. In medium bowl, mix eggs and milk. Pour cracker crumbs into another medium bowl. Dip meat into egg mixture, then into crumbs; coat evenly. In large skillet, heat oil over medium heat until hot. Cook steaks, turning once, 5 minutes or until evenly browned. Season with salt and pepper. Serve with gravy.

8 servings.

MANSEF (LAMB)

Asaf Hanoon
Arlington, Texas

1/2 cup olive oil
1 (31/2-lb.) boneless leg of lamb or
 lamb shoulder, cut into 1/2-inch
 cubes
4 large yellow onions, cubed
21/2 teaspoons salt
1 teaspoon freshly ground pepper
1 teaspoon paprika
1 teaspoon ground cumin
1 teaspoon mesquite
3 cups long-grain rice
1/4 lb. pine nuts, toasted

1. In large skillet, heat oil over medium-high heat until hot. Add lamb; brown on all sides. Remove lamb from skillet; set aside. Sauté onions about 5 minutes or until golden. Return lamb to skillet; season with salt, pepper, paprika, cumin and mesquite.

2. Add water just to cover meat; reduce heat to medium-low. Cook, uncovered, 11/2 to 2 hours or until lamb is very tender. Stir occasionally.

3. Transfer lamb and about 1 cup pan juices to covered bowl; keep warm in oven. Bring juices to a boil (if necessary, add water to make at least 5 cups liquid.); add rice. Cover and cook over low heat about 30 minutes or until rice is tender.

4. Arrange rice in middle of large serving plate; place lamb around rice and sprinkle with pine nuts. Garnish with parsley. Serve with rosemary baked potatoes and cheese burekas (Middle Eastern pastry).

8 servings.

LAMB-STUFFED EGGPLANT

Kathy Hickey
Ashley, Pennsylvania

1 medium eggplant
2 tablespoons vegetable oil
11/2 cups cooked cubed lamb
1 garlic clove, minced
1 small onion, chopped
1/2 cup chopped green bell pepper
1/4 cup chopped fresh parsley
1 cup cooked rice
1 cup stewed sliced tomatoes
1/2 teaspoon seasoned salt
1/8 teaspoon freshly ground pepper
1/2 teaspoon dried basil
1/4 teaspoon dried tarragon
1 teaspoon Worcestershire sauce
1/2 cup lamb gravy
1/2 cup boiling water

1. Heat oven to 350°F. Spray 2-quart casserole with nonstick cooking spray.

2. Cut eggplant in half lengthwise; remove pulp, leaving 1/2-inch shell. In large skillet, heat oil over medium-high heat until hot. Sauté pulp, lamb, garlic, onion, bell pepper and parsley 5 minutes. Stir in rice, tomatoes, salt, pepper, basil, tarragon, Worcestershire sauce and gravy. Bring to a boil and simmer 10 minutes, stirring occasionally.

3. Heap mixture into shells, rounding tops; place in casserole. Pour boiling water in casserole; bake 45 minutes.

2 to 4 servings.

Lamb Chops Bingo

LAMB CHOPS BINGO

Margaret Pache
Mesa, Arizona

4 lamb loin chops (1 inch thick)
$1/2$ cup fresh lime juice
1 tablespoon curry powder
1 teaspoon low-sodium soy sauce
$1/3$ cup Dijon mustard
$1/3$ cup honey
1 tablespoon cornstarch
2 tablespoons water
2 cups hot cooked rice
$1/4$ cup sliced green onions

1. Heat oven to 350°F. Arrange lamb chops in 3-quart casserole.

2. In small bowl, combine juice, curry, soy sauce, mustard and honey; whisk until well blended. Pour over lamb. Bake, uncovered, about 1 hour or until brown and tender. Baste frequently with sauce.

3. Meanwhile, combine cornstarch and water until smooth. When lamb is done, remove from pan and keep warm. Stir cornstarch mixture into sauce; heat briefly over low heat until thickened and clear. Spread rice on serving platter. Arrange lamb on rice; spoon sauce over lamb. Sprinkle with green onions.

4 servings.

LEG OF LAMB

Sylvia Prior
Culver City, California

1 (5- to 6-lb.) leg of lamb
4 large garlic cloves, quartered
 lengthwise
2 sprigs fresh rosemary or
 2 tablespoons dried
$1/2$ cup red wine vinegar
$1/4$ cup tablespoons all-purpose flour
1 cup water
$1/2$ teaspoon salt
$1/2$ teaspoon freshly ground pepper

1. Heat oven to 325°F.

2. Rinse lamb in cool water. Make 16 slits in lamb roast; insert one piece of garlic into each slit. Sprinkle rosemary over lamb.

3. Place lamb in large roaster; gently pour vinegar over lamb. Bake 2 to $2^{1}/_{2}$ hours or until internal temperature reaches 160°F. Let stand 10 minutes, tented with aluminum foil, before carving.

4. To make gravy, pour pan drippings from roaster into small saucepan. Stir in flour.

12 servings.

DILL PICKLE SAUCE MEATLOAF

Loretta Abrams
Phoenix, Arizona

2 lb. ground beef
1 medium onion, chopped
1 cup crushed butter crackers
$1/2$ cup dill pickle juice
1 egg
$1 1/2$ teaspoons salt
$1/4$ teaspoon freshly ground pepper
$1/2$ cup chopped dill pickles
$1/2$ cup ketchup
$1/4$ cup water
2 tablespoons sugar
1 teaspoon Worcestershire sauce

1. Heat oven to 350°F. Spray 9x5-inch loaf pan with nonstick cooking spray.

2. In medium bowl, combine beef, onion, crumbs, juice, egg, salt and pepper; mix well. Shape mixture into loaf pan.

3. In small bowl, combine pickles, ketchup, water, sugar and Worcestershire sauce; mix well. Spread mixture over loaf. Bake 40 minutes; baste twice. Bake an additional 35 minutes or until internal temperature reaches 160°F.

6 to 8 servings.

BARBECUED MEATLOAVES

Elaine Millsaps
Tampa, Florida

1 lb. lean ground beef
1 egg, lightly beaten
$1/4$ cup fine dry bread crumbs
1 tablespoon minced fresh parsley
2 tablespoons chopped onion
2 tablespoons horseradish
1 teaspoon salt
$1/8$ teaspoon freshly ground pepper
$1/4$ cup water
$1/2$ cup chili sauce
3 tablespoons ketchup
1 teaspoon Worcestershire sauce
$1/2$ teaspoon dry mustard
Dash hot pepper sauce

1. Heat oven to 350°F. Spray 3-quart casserole with nonstick cooking spray.

2. In large bowl, combine beef, egg, bread crumbs, parsley, onion, horseradish, salt, pepper and water; mix well. Shape into 4 oblong loaves. Arrange loaves in casserole about 1 inch apart.

3. In another large bowl, combine chili sauce, ketchup, Worcestershire sauce, mustard and hot pepper sauce. Spread mixture over tops and sides of loaves. Bake 45 minutes. Baste loaves 2 or 3 times until internal temperature reaches 160°F.

4 servings.

LULEH KABOB
Rawan Raza—Chino Hills, California

KABOBS
1 lb. ground beef or lamb
¹/₄ cup minced parsley
1 small onion, minced
1 teaspoon salt
¹/₂ teaspoon ground allspice
¹/₂ teaspoon freshly ground pepper
¹/₄ teaspoon ground cloves
1 tablespoon dry bread crumbs

SALAD
2 large red onions
2 tablespoons salt
1 bunch chopped parsley finely
2 tablespoons dried sumac*
¹/₄ teaspoon crushed red pepper
1 tablespoon fresh lemon juice
3 large ripe tomatoes
1 large onion
1 green bell pepper
¹/₈ teaspoon salt
¹/₈ teaspoon freshly ground pepper
1 tablespoon chopped parsley
1 tablespoon olive oil

1. In large bowl, combine beef, parsley, minced onion, salt, allspice, pepper, cloves and bread crumbs; mix well. Shape mixture into 4 (3-inch) "sausages." Thread skewer through each "sausage."

2. Heat grill. Place skewers on gas grill over medium-high heat or on charcoal grill 4 to 6 inches from medium coals. Cook 5 to 10 minutes, turning once, until beef is no longer pink in center.

3. Meanwhile, cut red onions into very thin, long slices. Sprinkle with salt and leave at room temperature 30 minutes. With hand, squeeze out juice and place onions in large bowl. Stir in parsley; season with sumac and red pepper. Transfer to serving bowl.

4. Heat broiler. Broil tomatoes, onion and bell pepper 4 to 6 inches from heat 5 minutes per side or until easy to peel. Peel and chop into small pieces. Combine vegetables in medium bowl with salt, pepper, parsley and olive oil; mix well. Serve salad with kabobs.

4 servings.

TIP *Dried sumac is available in Greek or Middle Eastern markets.

BAKED ALASKA MEATLOAF
Elaine Millsaps—Tampa, Florida

2 lb. lean ground beef
2 eggs, slightly beaten
1 teaspoons salt
¹/₂ teaspoon freshly ground pepper
1¹/₂ cups fresh bread crumbs
¹/₄ cup minced onion
1¹/₂ teaspoons minced fresh oregano
   or ¹/₂ teaspoon dried
1¹/₂ teaspoons minced fresh sweet
   basil or ¹/₂ teaspoon dried
4 cups prepared mashed potatoes
¹/₄ (1-oz.) cup freshly grated
   Parmesan cheese
¹/₄ teaspoon papriks

1. Heat oven to 350°F. In large bowl, combine beef, eggs, salt, pepper, bread crumbs, onion, oregano and basil; mix well. Pack firmly into greased 1-quart round ovenproof bowl. Bake 1 hour and 20 minutes.

2. Drain off excess liquid; invert bowl onto wire rack to drain completely. Pat loaf dry with paper towels. Slide loaf onto rimmed baking sheet. Frost meat loaf with potatoes. Sprinkle with Parmesan cheese and paprika. Bake an additional 25 to 30 minutes or until surface is golden brown.

6 servings.

MARVELOUS MEATLOAF

Jennifer Maxwell
Springfield, Missouri

2 lb. ground beef
1 (1-oz.) pkg. onion soup mix
³/₄ cup crushed butter crackers
1 egg
1 chopped onion
1 cup (4 oz.) shredded cheddar cheese
¹/₂ cup ketchup

1. Heat oven to 350°F. Spray 9x5-inch loaf pan with nonstick cooking spray.

2. In large bowl, combine beef, soup mix, crackers, egg and onion; mix well. Shape half of the mixture into pan. Make well in center. Place cheese in well; top with remaining mixture. Drizzle with ketchup. Bake 1 to 1¹/₄ hours or until internal temperature reaches 160°F.

6 to 8 servings.

RIPE OLIVE HAM LOAF

Lucy Kelly
Scottsdale, Arizona

1 cup canned pitted ripe olives,
  drained, coarsely chopped
2 eggs
1 cup fresh bread crumbs
³/₄ cup milk
¹/₄ cup minced onion
2 teaspoons mustard
1 lb. lean ground ham
1 lb. lean ground pork

1. Heat oven to 350°F. Spray 9x5-inch loaf pan with nonstick cooking spray.

2. In large bowl, beat eggs at medium speed until frothy. Stir in bread crumbs, milk, onion and mustard; mix well. Stir in meat and olives; mix well. Shape mixture into loaf pan. Bake 1¹/₄ hours or until internal temperature reaches 160°F. Serve hot or cold.

6 servings.

OUR FAMILY'S FAVORITE MEATLOAF

Charlotte Ward
Hilton Head Island, South Carolina

¹/₂ lb. ground beef
¹/₂ lb. ground veal
¹/₂ lb. ground pork
2 cups fresh bread crumbs, cubed
1 cup milk
1 egg, beaten
1 tablespoon Worcestershire sauce
¹/₄ cup minced onion
1¹/₄ teaspoons salt
¹/₄ teaspoon freshly ground pepper
¹/₄ teaspoon dry mustard
¹/₄ teaspoon dried sage
¹/₄ teaspoon celery salt
¹/₄ teaspoon garlic salt
3 tablespoons ketchup

1. Heat oven to 350°F. Spray 9x5-inch loaf pan with nonstick cooking spray.

2. In large bowl, combine beef, veal, pork and bread cubes; mix well. In another large bowl, combine milk, egg and Worcestershire sauce; mix well. Pour milk mixture into beef mixture; mix well.

3. In small bowl, combine onion, salt, pepper, mustard, sage, celery salt and garlic salt; mix well. Stir into meat mixture.

4. Form mixture into loaf pan; drizzle with ketchup. Bake 1 hour 15 minutes or until internal temperature reaches 160°F.

6 servings.

Our Family's Favorite Meat Loaf

GREEK SAUSAGES IN MINT SAUCE

Kathy Hickey
Ashley, Pennsylvania

1$^{1}/_{4}$ lb. lean ground beef
$^{1}/_{4}$ cup chopped onion
$^{1}/_{2}$ cup fresh bread crumbs
1 egg, beaten
$^{1}/_{4}$ cup milk
1 garlic clove, minced
1$^{1}/_{2}$ teaspoons dried oregano
1$^{1}/_{2}$ teaspoons dried mint
1 teaspoon salt
$^{1}/_{4}$ teaspoon freshly ground pepper
2 tablespoons butter
1 (8-oz.) can tomato sauce
$^{1}/_{2}$ cup water
$^{1}/_{2}$ teaspoon sugar
$^{1}/_{8}$ teaspoon garlic salt

1. In large bowl, combine beef and onion; mix well. In medium bowl, combine bread crumbs, egg, milk, garlic and seasonings; mix well. Add bread crumb mixture to beef mixture; mix thoroughly. Shape into fat "sausages" about 2$^{1}/_{2}$ inches long.

2. In large skillet, melt butter over medium heat; add sausages. Lightly brown meat on all sides. In another bowl, combine tomato sauce, water, sugar and garlic salt; mix well. Pour mixture over meat; simmer 20 to 30 minutes or until no longer pink in center and internal temperature reaches 160°F. If sauce is too thick, add a little water. Serve over rice or noodles, if desired.

4 servings.

VEAL MEATBALLS IN PORT SAUCE

Ronald J. Harrigan
New York, New York

1 (14.5-oz.) can reduced-sodium
   chicken broth
1 (14.5-oz.) can reduced-sodium
   beef broth
$^{2}/_{3}$ cup port wine
2$^{1}/_{2}$ tablespoons butter
2$^{1}/_{2}$ tablespoons all-purpose flour
$^{1}/_{8}$ teaspoon salt
$^{1}/_{8}$ teaspoon freshly ground pepper
$^{1}/_{8}$ teaspoon sugar
1 lb. ground veal
2 large egg yolks
$^{1}/_{2}$ cup dry bread crumbs
5 tablespoons freshly grated pecorino-
   Romano cheese

1. In large bowl combine broths. In small saucepan, bring 3 cups of the broth and port to a boil over medium heat. Remove from heat; keep warm.

2. In large saucepan, melt butter over medium heat. Stir in flour until smooth. Add broth-port mixture, salt, pepper and sugar. Stir and simmer 4 to 5 minutes or until slightly thickened and smooth. Keep warm.

3. In food processor, combine veal, yolks, bread crumbs, cheese and 4 to 5 tablespoons remaining broth-port mixture. Season with salt, if desired. Blend well 1 minute. Remove mixture to clean bowl; shape into 30 meat balls about 1$^{1}/_{2}$ inches in diameter.

4. Return sauce to a simmer. Add meatballs; simmer 4 to 6 minutes or until firm and no longer pink in center.

4 servings.

BY FISH OR BY SEA

CURRIED RED SNAPPER

Tammy Raynes
Natchitoches, Louisiana

1¹/₂ lb. fresh red snapper fillets
1 tablespoon margarine, softened
2 medium onions, chopped
2 ribs celery, chopped
1 teaspoon curry powder
³/₄ teaspoon salt
¹/₄ cup milk

1. Heat oven to 350°F. Spray 13x9-inch pan with nonstick cooking spray.

2. Arrange fillets in pan.

3. In large skillet, melt butter over medium heat. Sauté onions and celery until tender. Stir in curry and salt; mix well. Remove skillet from heat; stir in milk.

4. Spoon mixture over fillets. Bake, uncovered, 25 minutes or until fish flakes easily with fork.

4 to 6 servings.

SOLE IN HERBED BUTTER

Tammy Raynes
Natchitoches, Louisiana

¹/₄ cup butter, softened
1 teaspoon dried dill weed
¹/₂ teaspoon onion powder
¹/₂ teaspoon garlic powder
¹/₂ teaspoon salt
¹/₄ teaspoon ground white pepper
2 lb. sole

1. In small bowl, combine butter, dill, onion powder, garlic powder, salt and pepper; mix well.

2. In large skillet, heat mixture over medium heat until butter is melted. Sauté fish 3 to 5 minutes per side or until fish flakes easily with fork. Garnish with dill and lemon.

6 to 8 servings.

MILFORD'S GREEK SAUTE

Deanna Jones
Parker, Colorado

¹/₄ cup butter
6 oz. fresh ahi (yellowfin tuna), cut into ¹/₂-inch chunks
²/₃ cup sliced mushrooms
¹/₄ cup sliced ripe olives
1 cup diced tomatoes
1 teaspoon minced garlic
1 teaspoon dried basil
2 tablespoons white wine
2 green onions, diced
3 tablespoons feta cheese, crumbled

1. In small skillet, melt butter over medium heat. Sauté tuna and mushrooms until tender.

2. Stir in olives, tomatoes, garlic, basil and wine; sauté until fish flakes easily with fork. Sprinkle with green onions and cheese. Serve over rice, if desired. Garnish with parsley and lemon.

1 to 2 servings.

Milford's Greek Saute

ZESTY DILLY SALMON

Joseph Barry
Burbank, Illinois

1 (³/₄-lb.) salmon fillet, halved
¹/₂ cup sour cream
1 teaspoon dried dill weed
¹/₄ teaspoon garlic powder
¹/₈ teaspoon salt
¹/₈ teaspoon freshly ground pepper
1 green bell pepper, cut into wedges
1 red bell pepper, cut into wedges
1 lemon, sliced

1. Heat oven to 425°F.

2. Place each fillet on 18x24-inch piece of aluminum foil. Lightly cover with sour cream. Season with dill, garlic powder, salt and pepper. Place peppers around fish and 2 to 3 lemon slices on each fillet.

3. Fold foil to form large packets, leaving room for heat circulation. Place packets on baking sheet. Bake 20 to 25 minutes or until fish flakes easily with fork.

2 servings.

SALMON CARLOTTA

Charlotte Ward
Hilton Head Island, South Carolina

4 teaspoons Dijon mustard
3 tablespoons packed brown sugar
1 teaspoon low-sodium soy sauce
1 teaspoon rice vinegar
1 teaspoon lemon pepper
1 teaspoon dill seed
1 lb. salmon fillet (1-inch thick)

1. Heat broiler.

2. In large bowl, combine mustard, brown sugar, soy sauce, vinegar, lemon pepper and dill; mix well. Set aside. Rinse salmon in cold water and dry with paper towels.

3. Broil salmon skin side down 4 to 6 inches from heat 8 minutes or until fish flakes easily with fork. Brush glaze over fillet; broil an additional 2 minutes. Drizzle remaining glaze over salmon before serving.

4 servings.

FISH IN CHIPS

Joseph Barry–Burbank, Illinois

1 cup crushed plain potato chips
¹/₄ teaspoon ground celery seed
¹/₄ teaspoon dried thyme
2¹/₄ tablespoons unsalted butter
1 lb. fresh white fish fillets, cut into
    8 pieces
¹/₈ teaspoon salt
¹/₈ teaspoon freshly ground pepper

1. Heat oven to 450°F. Spray 13x9-inch pan with nonstick cooking spray.

2. Place crushed chips on large plate. Add celery seeds and thyme; stir lightly with fork.

3. In large skillet, melt butter over low heat. Remove skillet from heat. Dip each piece of fish in butter, then roll in chips. Press chips into fish. Arrange fillets in pan about 1 inch apart. Season with salt and pepper. Drizzle remaining melted butter over fish.

4. Bake fillets 7 to 8 minutes until coating is golden brown and fish flakes easily with fork. Serve immediately.

4 servings.

BAKED TROUT

Tammy Raynes
Natchitoches, Louisiana

1 (8-oz.) pkg. sliced fresh mushrooms
$1/2$ cup margarine, melted
1 cup fresh bread crumbs
$1/8$ teaspoon salt
$1/8$ teaspoon freshly ground pepper
4 (4-oz.) trout fillets

1. Heat oven to 375°F.

2. Place mushrooms in 11x7-inch baking dish. Drizzle with 2 tablespoons of the margarine; set aside.

3. In medium bowl, combine bread crumbs, salt and pepper; stir well.

4. Dip fillets in 3 tablespoons of the margarine, then dredge in crumb mixture.

5. Place fillets on top of mushrooms. Drizzle with remaining 3 tablespoons margarine. Bake, uncovered, 20 minutes or until fish flakes easily with fork.

4 servings.

CHEESE SALMON LOAF

Marianne Lavella
Lady Lake, Florida

1 ($14^3/4$-oz.) can pink boneless
  salmon, drained
$1 1/4$ cups (5 oz.) shredded Muenster
  or other mild white cheese
1 egg
$1/2$ cup heavy cream, whipped
$1/2$ teaspoon salt
1 $1/3$ cups dry bread crumbs
3 tablespoons butter, melted
1 tablespoon dried parsley
1 tablespoon fresh lemon juice
$1/8$ teaspoon freshly ground pepper

1. Heat oven to 350°F. Spray 8x4-inch loaf pan with nonstick cooking spray.

2. In large bowl, combine salmon, cheese, egg, cream, salt, 1 cup of the bread crumbs, butter, parsley, lemon juice and pepper; mix well.

3. Spoon mixture lightly into loaf pan. Sprinkle remaining $1/3$ cup bread crumbs over loaf. Bake 45 minutes to 1 hour or until lightly browned.

6 to 8 servings.

MACADAMIA SCALLOPED MAHI MAHI

Nancy Suske–Kailua, Hawaii

$1/2$ cup butter, melted
1 cup crushed butter crackers
1 tablespoon dried parsley or 2
  tablespoons fresh
$1/2$ teaspoon salt
Dash freshly ground pepper
$3/4$ cup chopped macadamia nuts
1 lb. mahi mahi
$1/3$ cup half-and-half

1. In large bowl, combine butter, crumbs, parsley, salt, pepper and nuts; mix well.

2. In $1 1/2$-quart casserole, arrange mahi mahi skin side down. Cover with plastic wrap, leaving 1 corner open. Microwave at high power 4 minutes. Turn fish over; sprinkle with crumb mixture. Pour in half-and-half.

3. Return casserole to microwave; cook an additional 4 to 5 minutes or until fish flakes easily with fork. Let stand 5 minutes before serving.

4 servings.

Chesapeake Bay Crab Cakes with Jalapeno Tartar Sauce

CHESAPEAKE BAY CRAB CAKES WITH JALAPENO TARTAR SAUCE

David A. Heppner
Brandon, Florida

SAUCE
1/2 cup reduced-fat mayonnaise
1 small jalapeño chile, seeded, finely
   chopped
3 tablespoons finely chopped English
   cucumber
2 tablespoons finely chopped red
   onion
1 tablespoon fresh lemon juice
1/4 teaspoon Worcestershire sauce

CAKES
2 large eggs, lightly beaten
2 tablespoons reduced-fat mayonnaise
2 tablespoons finely chopped green
   bell pepper
1 (2-oz.) jar diced pimientos, drained
1 1/2 tablespoons finely chopped red
   onion
1 1/2 teaspoons fresh lemon juice
1 teaspoon Dijon mustard
1/2 teaspoon Old Bay seasoning
1/2 cup fresh whole-grain bread crumbs
1 lb. lump crabmeat, drained, flaked

1. In large bowl, combine mayonnaise, jalapeño, cucumber, onion, lemon juice and Worcestershire sauce; mix well. Cover and refrigerate 1 to 2 hours.

2. In another large bowl, combine eggs, mayonnaise, green bell pepper, pimientos, onion, lemon juice, mustard and Old Bay seasoning; mix well. Fold in bread crumbs and crabmeat. Divide mixture into 12 portions; shape each portion into 3-inch patty.

3. Spray large skillet with nonstick cooking spray. Heat skillet over medium-high heat until hot; add crab cakes. Cook 3 to 4 minutes or until golden brown, turning once. Serve crab cakes hot, topped with small dollop of sauce. Garnish with peppers, sprouts and lemon wedges.

4 servings.

BAKED ORANGE ROUGHY

Tammy Raynes
Natchitoches, Louisiana

1 1/2 lb. orange roughy fillets
2 egg whites
3/4 cup mayonnaise
1 teaspoon curry powder

1. Heat oven to 350°F. Spray 13x9-inch pan with nonstick cooking spray.

2. Place fillets in pan; set aside.

3. In medium bowl, beat egg whites at medium speed until soft peaks form. Gently fold in mayonnaise and curry powder. Spread mixture evenly over fillets. Bake 25 to 30 minutes or until fish flakes easily with fork. Serve immediately.

4 to 6 servings.

SALMON CROQUETTES

Deborah Selig
Medford, Oregon

36 butter crackers, crushed
1 (16-oz.) can salmon, shredded
1 egg, beaten
1/8 teaspoon freshly ground pepper
1/8 teaspoon garlic salt
1 tablespoon fresh lemon juice
1/4 cup oil

1. In medium bowl, combine half the cracker crumbs, salmon, egg, pepper, garlic salt and lemon juice; mix well. Roll mixture into 1/2-inch croquettes, then roll balls in crumbs.

2. In large skillet, heat oil over medium-high heat until hot. Fry croquettes until evenly browned.

12 croquettes.

CRAWFISH ETOUFEE

Tammy Raynes
Natchitoches, Louisiana

1 cup margarine
2 medium onions, chopped
$^1/_2$ garlic clove, chopped
1 large green bell pepper, chopped
1 lb. shelled crawfish
$^1/_8$ teaspoon salt
$^1/_8$ teaspoon freshly ground pepper
$^1/_8$ teaspoon cayenne pepper
2 (8-oz.) cans tomato sauce

1. Melt $^1/_2$ cup of the margarine in large skillet over medium-high heat. Sauté onion, garlic and bell pepper. Sauté until onions are tender.

2. Reduce heat to low; add crawfish and sauté until pink. Season with salt, pepper and cayenne. Stir in tomato sauce and remaining $^1/_2$ cup margarine. Simmer 40 minutes. Serve over hot cooked rice, if desired.

2 to 4 servings.

BAKED FISH FILLETS

Z. Burt Parker
Urbana, Illinois

1 medium onion, sliced
2 cups sliced carrots
1 ($10^3/_4$-oz.) can condensed cream of
  celery soup
$^1/_4$ cup butter, softened
1 tablespoon minced fresh parsley
$^1/_8$ teaspoon salt
$^1/_8$ teaspoon freshly ground pepper
2 lb. fish fillets

1. Heat oven to 400°F.

2. In small bowl, combine onion, carrots, soup, butter, parsley, salt and pepper; mix well.

3. Divide fillets into 6 portions; place each fillet on sheet of lightly-oiled aluminum foil. Place equal portions of vegetable mixture over each fillet; close package, double folding all edges. Place packets in 3-quart casserole. Bake 30 minutes or until fish flakes easily with fork.

6 servings.

MUSSELS MAGNIFIQUE

Sherry Lynn Rothstein–Mandeville, Lousiana

$1^1/_2$ tablespoons butter
3 shallots, chopped
1 medium yellow onion, diced
1 tablespoon fresh lemon juice
$^1/_8$ teaspoon salt
$^1/_8$ teaspoon freshly ground pepper
$^1/_2$ cup water
1 (750 ml) bottle Sauvignon Blanc
3 lb. fresh mussels
$1^1/_2$ cups chopped fresh parsley
1 small tomato, chopped

1. In Dutch oven, melt butter over medium-high heat. Sauté shallots and onion until onion is transparent. Add lemon juice, salt, pepper, water and wine; bring to a simmer. Stir in mussels; cook, covered, until mussels open. If liquid starts to boil over, set cover slightly ajar. Remove from heat. Stir in 1 cup of the parsley.

2. Divide mixture among individual bowls; garnish with tomato and remaining $^1/_2$ cup parsley. Transfer liquid to large dipping bowl. Serve with sliced French bread, if desired.

2 to 4 servings.

Mussels Magnifique

SHRIMP CREOLE

Gloria Snyder
Schnecksville, Pennsylvania

¼ cup vegetable oil
¼ cup all-purpose flour
½ cup chopped onion
¼ cup chopped celery
1 (8-oz.) can tomato sauce
1 tablespoon chopped fresh parsley
1½ lb. shelled, deveined uncooked
   medium shrimp
½ cup cooking sherry
½ teaspoon freshly ground pepper
¼ teaspoon crushed red pepper
Hot cooked rice

1. In large skillet, heat oil over medium-high heat until hot. Stir flour into oil; cook until brown. Stir in onion and celery; Cook until tender. Stir in tomato sauce and parsley; cook 10 minutes.

2. Stir in shrimp, sherry, pepper and red pepper; cook about 10 minutes. If sauce is too thick, add ½ cup water after sherry. Serve over rice.

4 to 6 servings.

LAZY STUFFED SHRIMP WITH RICE PILAF

Douglas Tates
Stroudsberg, Pennsylvania

PILAF
2 tablespoons butter
2 tablespoons olive oil
½ cup chopped onion
1½ cups rice
3 chicken bouillon cubes
3 cups boiling water
½ teaspoon salt
2 tablespoons chopped fresh parsley

SHRIMP
1 lb. shelled, deveined uncooked
   medium shrimp
¼ cup butter
¾ cup dry bread crumbs
2 garlic cloves, minced

1. To make pilaf, melt butter in large skillet over medium-high heat; add oil. Sauté onions until soft; reduce heat to low. Stir in rice; sauté until grains are golden.

2. In large saucepan, dissolve bouillon cubes in water; add to rice mixture. Add salt; cover and bring to a boil. Reduce heat to low; simmer 18 minutes without stirring. Remove cover; stir and cook until all liquid is absorbed. Fluff rice with fork. Sprinkle with parsley, if desired.

3. To make shrimp, melt butter in large skillet. Sauté garlic over medium-high heat until fragrant; add shrimp. As shrimp turn pink, add bread crumbs. Keep moist and serve over rice pilaf.

4 servings.

SEAFOOD CASSEROLE

David A. Heppner
Brandon, Florida

$^1/_4$ cup all-purpose flour
$^1/_3$ cup minced onion
$^1/_4$ cup butter
1 cup milk
1 cup half-and-half
$^1/_2$ teaspoon salt
$^1/_2$ teaspoon freshly ground pepper
1 tablespoon diced pimientos
1 (8-oz.) can sliced water chestnuts, drained
2 tablespoons fresh lemon juice
1 tablespoon chopped fresh parsley
1 cup cooked crabmeat
1 cup shelled, deveined medium shrimp
3 cups hot cooked rice
1 cup (4 oz.) shredded cheddar cheese

1. In large skillet, melt butter over medium-high heat. Sauté onion until tender. Stir in flour, milk and half-and-half; cook and stir until thick and bubbly. Remove from heat. Add salt, pepper, pimientos, water chestnuts, lemon juice, parsley, crabmeat, shrimp, rice and $^1/_2$ cup of the cheese to skillot.

2. Spoon mixture into 2$^1/_2$-quart casserole. Sprinkle remaining $^1/_2$ cup cheese over casserole just before serving.

6 servings.

CLAMS CONSTANTINO

Suzanne Stewart
Lauderdale Lakes, Florida

1 (16-oz.) can black beans
1 tablespoon oil
8 green onions, chopped
3 tablespoons finely diced onion
1 tablespoon chopped garlic
36 fresh small clams

1. In large bowl, mash half of the black beans. Combine mashed beans with remaining unmashed beans; set aside.

2. In large skillet, heat oil over medium-high heat until hot. Sauté half of the green onions and onion 2 to 3 minutes or until tender. Add garlic; simmer 1 minute. Remove from heat; mix in beans, stirring occasionally.

3. In large pot, steam clams just until they open. Discard any clams that do not open. Drain and place clams on heated dish. Pour bean mixture over clams; sprinkle with remaining green onions. Serve with bread or tortillas and salsa, if desired.

4 servings.

Garlic Shrimp with Salsa Verde

GARLIC SHRIMP WITH SALSA VERDE

Ellen Quigg
Springfield, Ontario

SALSA
1 small onion, finely chopped
6 tablespoons fresh lime juice
1 cup finely chopped fresh cilantro
2 garlic cloves, minced
2 tablespoons vegetable oil
$1/2$ cup chopped fresh parsley
3 tablespoons white vinegar
1 jalapeño chile, seeded, minced

SHRIMP
$1/4$ cup vegetable oil
12 garlic cloves, roughly chopped
$1^1/2$ lb. shelled, deveined uncooked
  medium shrimp
2 tablespoons butter

1. In large bowl, combine onion, lime juice, cilantro, garlic, oil, parsley, vinegar and jalapeño; mix well. Cover and refrigerate overnight or up to 24 hours.

2. In large skillet, heat oil over medium-high heat until hot. Sauté garlic 6 to 8 minutes or until brown. Quickly whisk in butter; immediately remove from heat. Remove garlic pieces with slotted spoon; reserve.

3. To prepare shrimp, heat reserved oil in another large skillet over medium-high heat until hot; sauté until shrimp turn pink. Serve with Salsa. Garnish with browned garlic pieces.

4 to 6 servings.

SEAFOOD GUMBO

Tammy Raynes
Natchitoches, Louisiana

1 tablespoon vegetable oil
$1/2$ cup sliced celery
$1/2$ cup chopped onion
$1/2$ cup chopped green bell pepper
1 garlic clove, minced
1 (14.5-oz.) can reduced-sodium
  chicken broth
1 (14.5-oz.) can diced tomatoes
2 cups sliced fresh okra
$3/4$ cup chili sauce
$1/2$ teaspoon salt
$1/4$ teaspoon freshly ground pepper
$1/4$ teaspoon dried thyme
1 bay leaf
Dash hot pepper sauce
1 lb. shrimp or other seafood
$1^1/3$ cups hot cooked rice

1. In medium saucepan, heat oil over medium-high heat until hot. Sauté celery, onions, bell pepper and garlic until tender. Add broth, tomatoes, okra, chili sauce, salt, pepper, thyme, bay leaf and hot pepper sauce. Simmer, covered, 20 minutes.

2. Add shrimp to saucepan; simmer, covered, 15 to 20 minutes or until shrimp turn pink. Remove bay leaf. Place $1/3$ cup rice in individual bowl; top with gumbo.

4 servings.

SEAFOOD MORNAY

Cathy Miller
Ringwood, New Jersey

1/2 cup butter
1/4 cup all-purpose flour
1 cup half-and-half
1/2 cup reduced-sodium chicken broth
1/2 cup white wine
1/4 teaspoon cayenne pepper
1/2 teaspoon salt
1/4 teaspoon freshly ground pepper
1/4 teaspoon nutmeg
3 cups (12-oz.) shredded Swiss cheese
2 lb. shelled, deveined uncooked
    medium shrimp

1. Heat oven to 375°F. Spray 3-quart casserole with nonstick cooking spray.

2. In large skillet, melt 1/4 cup of the butter over medium-high heat; blend in flour. Cook until smooth, stirring occasionally, but do not brown. Remove from heat. Whisk in half-and-half, stock and wine. Return to heat and bring to a boil; cook 1 to 2 minutes or until thick. Stir in cayenne, salt, pepper, nutmeg and 2 1/2 cups of the cheese. Remove from heat; stir until cheese melts.

3. In another large skillet, sauté shrimp in remaining 1/4 cup butter until shrimp turn pink. Add sauce to seafood. Pour mixture into individual casserole dishes; top with remaining 1/2 cup cheese. Bake until browned and bubbly. Serve with salad and rice pilaf, if desired.

4 servings.

SEAFOOD CASSEROLE

Stacey Caffrey
Lafayette, Louisiana

3 tablespoons butter
2 tablespoons all-purpose flour
3 cups milk
3 eggs, beaten
1 teaspoon salt
Dash nutmeg
1/4 cup cooking sherry
12 fresh oysters*
2 cups shelled, deveined uncooked
    medium shrimp
1 cup uncooked crabmeat
1 lb. uncooked crawfish
1/2 cup dry bread crumbs
1 cup (4 oz.) grated mozzarella cheese
1/4 cup chopped fresh parsley
1/8 teaspoon paprika

1. Heat oven to 325°F. Spray 2-quart casserole with nonstick cooking spray.

2. In large skillet, melt butter over medium-high heat. Stir in flour, milk, eggs, salt and nutmeg. Cook until thick; stir in sherry. Set aside.

3. Combine oysters, shrimp, crabmeat and crawfish in casserole; toss gently. Pour flour mixture over seafood. Sprinkle with bread crumbs, cheese, parsley and paprika.

4. Bake, uncovered, 25 minutes or until shrimp turn pink.

4 to 6 servings.

TIP *Oysters may be omitted, in which case more shrimp, crawfish or diced cooked eggplant can be added.

SCALLOPS WITH ORANGE-FLAVORED LIQUEUR AND ANGEL HAIR PASTA

Charlotte Ward
Hilton Head Island, South Carolina

3 tablespoons unsalted butter
1 lb. sea scallops, halved
1/8 teaspoon salt
1/8 teaspoon freshly ground pepper
1/2 cup minced shallots
1 1/2 cups reduced-sodium chicken broth
1/2 cup dry white wine
1/4 cup fresh orange juice
1 cup sour cream
1/4 cup orange-flavored liqueur
1 teaspoon grated orange peel
8 oz. angel hair pasta
1 1/2 teaspoons fresh lemon juice

1. In large skillet, melt 1 1/2 tablespoons of the butter over medium-high heat; add scallops. Season with salt and pepper. Cook scallops 1 minute, stirring constantly. Cover and continue cooking, stirring occasionally, an additional 2 minutes or until scallops are opaque and just firm. With slotted spoon, transfer scallops to large plate. Cover and keep warm.

2. Add shallots to skillet; cook 1 minute, stirring constantly. Add broth, wine and orange juice. Boil mixture until reduced to 2/3 cup.

3. When broth mixture is reduced to 2/3 cup, stir in sour cream. Reduce heat to low; simmer until lightly thickened. Over medium-high heat, whisk in remaining butter, liqueur, orange peel and lemon juice. Pour scallops and any excess juices into sauce; simmer 3 minutes. Serve over pasta; sprinkle with stuffing and grated cheese, if desired.

4 servings.

SCALLOP PASTA DELIGHT

Michelle Arney
Scottsburg, New York

4 cups water
8 oz. farfalle (bow-tie pasta)
1 tablespoon kosher (coarse) salt
1 teaspoon olive oil
1 small garlic clove, sliced
1/2 lb. scallops
1/2 cup white wine
1 vegetable bouillon cube
2 teaspoons chopped fresh parsley
1 (4-oz.) can chopped mushroom, drained
1 (6-oz.) jar marinated artichoke hearts
1 teaspoon freshly ground pepper
1 teaspoon Old Bay seasoning
1 teaspoon seasoned salt
2 tablespoons grated pecorino cheese

1. In large saucepan, heat oil over medium-high heat until hot. Reduce heat to medium; gently sauté garlic until fragrant. Add scallops before garlic browns; sauté 5 minutes. Add wine, bouillon, parsley, mushrooms, artichokes, half of the artichoke marinade, pepper, Old Bay seasoning and salt; reduce heat to medium-low. Stir and cook until scallops are opaque.

2. Add pasta to saucepan. Stir and cook an additional 5 minutes. Serve in pasta bowls topped with pecorino cheese. Serve with bread, if desired.

2 servings.

HAWAIIAN SHRIMP KABOBS

Tammy Raynes
Natchitoches, Louisiana

1 (16-oz.) can pineapple juice
$^1/_3$ cup packed brown sugar
4 teaspoons cornstarch
1 tablespoon rice vinegar
1 tablespoon low-sodium soy sauce
1 garlic clove, minced
$^1/_4$ teaspoon ground ginger
1 green bell pepper, cut into
   1-inch squares
1 red bell pepper, cut into 1-inch
   squares
1 large onion, cut unto 1-inch squares
1 cup pineapple chunks
1 medium mango or papaya, cut into
   1-inch chunks
1 lb. shelled, deveined uncooked large
   shrimp
$2^1/_2$ cups hot cooked rice

1. Heat broiler. Spray rack of broiler pan with non-stick cooking spray.

2. In large saucepan, combine juice, brown sugar, cornstarch, vinegar, soy sauce, garlic and ginger; heat over medium heat until boiling and sauce thickens, Stirring frequently.

3. Alternately thread vegetables, fruits and shrimp on 10 metal skewers; brush with sauce. Place kabobs on broiler rack. Broil 4 to 6 inches from heat about 3 minutes. Turn and brush with sauce; broil an additional 3 minutes or until shrimp are pink. Serve with rice. Garnish with fresh herbs.

4 servings.

SPICY SHRIMP CASSEROLE

David A. Heppner
Brandon, Florida

3 cups cooked long-grain and wild
   rice mix
2 lb. shelled, deveined uncooked
   medium shrimp
1 cup (4 oz.) shredded longhorn
   cheddar cheese
1 ($10^3/_4$-oz.) can condensed cream of
   mushroom soup
1 tablespoon butter
$^1/_2$ cup chopped green onion
2 teaspoons Worcestershire sauce
$^1/_2$ teaspoon dry mustard
$^1/_2$ teaspoon freshly ground pepper
$^1/_4$ cup milk
1 teaspoon Cajun seasoning

1. Heat oven to 375°F. Spray 11x7-inch pan with nonstick cooking spray.

2. In large bowl, combine rice and shrimp; toss gently. Add cheese and soup; mix well.

3. In large skillet, melt butter over medium-high heat; sauté onion until tender. Stir onions into rice mixture.

4. Stir Worcestershire sauce, mustard, pepper, milk and Cajun seasoning into rice mixture; mix well. Spoon mixture into pan. Bake 45 minutes or until shrimp turn pink.

6 servings.

COMFORTING
ONE-DISH DINNERS

HOMEMADE POTATO SOUP

Judy Linder
Collins, Ohio

6 potatoes, peeled, cut into 1-inch
   pieces
2 onions, chopped
1 carrot, sliced
1 rib celery, sliced
4 chicken bouillon cubes
1 tablespoon chopped fresh parsley
5 cups water
1 tablespoon salt
$^1/_8$ teaspoon freshly ground pepper
$^1/_3$ cup butter
1 (12-oz.) can evaporated milk
$^1/_4$ cup chopped chives

1. In slow cooker, combine potatoes, onions, carrot, celery, bouillon, parsley, water, salt, pepper and butter; toss gently. Cover and cook on low heat setting 10 to 12 hours (or on high heat setting 3 to 4 hours). Stir in milk and chives during last hour.

4 to 6 servings.

SCALLOPED POTATOES AND SAUSAGE

Denise Hanson
Worthing, South Dakota

1 ($10^3/_4$ cup-oz.) can condensed
   cream of mushroom soup
4 lb. round white boiling potatoes,
   peeled, sliced
$^1/_4$ cup teaspoon salt
$^1/_2$ cup teaspoon freshly ground pepper
1 lb. smoked bratwurst, cut into
   1-inch pieces
$^1/_2$ cup cup milk
2 tablespoons butter, chopped

1. Heat oven to 350°F. Spray 13x9-inch pan with nonstick cooking spray.

2. In large bowl, combine potatoes, soup, salt and pepper; mix well. Add bratwurst; toss gently. Pour mixture into pan. Pour milk over bratwurst; top with butter. Cover with aluminum foil. Bake 1 hour or until potatoes are tender.

6 servings.

WHITMAN COUNTY SPLIT PEA SOUP

Walleen Hopkins–Sandy, Oregon

1 lb. split peas
2 large ribs celery, chopped
1 large carrot, chopped
1 large onion, chopped
1 ($1^1/_2$ lb.) ham hock
2 quarts boiling water
2 bay leaves
Dash cayenne pepper
$^1/_8$ teaspoon salt
$^1/_8$ teaspoon freshly ground pepper
1 teaspoon steak sauce
$^1/_2$ cup teaspoon dried thyme

1. In large pot, combine peas, celery, carrot, onion, ham, water, bay leaves, cayenne, salt, pepper and steak sauce; toss gently. Boil over medium heat 25 minutes. Reduce heat; simmer until peas are soft. Add thyme during last 20 minutes. Discard bay leaf. Reheat and serve hot.

8 to 12 servings.

ITALIAN TOMATO STEW

Sue Kimes
Overland, Missouri

3 tablespoons extra-virgin olive oil
1 lb. stew meat
¼ cup butter
2 to 3 lb. plum tomatoes, peeled
1 cup baby carrots
4 to 5 large red potatoes, peeled
1 bay leaf
1 teaspoon dried basil
1 teaspoon dried thyme
1 tablespoon oregano
1 teaspoon minced garlic
1 (8-oz.) can tomato sauce
4 ribs celery, coarsely chopped
1 cup sliced portobello mushrooms
½ cup diced onions
1 cup cut green beans
½ cup chopped shallots or leek
½ large head green cabbage
4 to 5 cups water
⅛ teaspoon salt
⅛ teaspoon freshly ground pepper
½ cup red wine

1. In large skillet, heat oil over medium-high heat until hot. Add butter; brown meat in butter and oil; add tomatoes, carrots, potatoes, bay leaf, basil, thyme, oregano, garlic, tomato sauce, celery, mushrooms, onions, green beans, shallots, cabbage, water, salt, pepper and wine.

2. Remove mixture to Dutch oven. Cook over low heat, covered, 1½ to 2 hours or until vegetables are tender.

10 to 12 servings.

SPAGHETTI PIE

Carole Anne Barbaro
Clayton, New Jersey

6 oz. spaghetti
2 tablespoons butter
⅓ cup (1½ oz.) freshly grated
  Parmesan cheese
2 eggs, beaten
1 cup (4 oz.) ricotta cheese
1 (32-oz.) can tomato sauce
½ cup (2 oz.) mozzarella cheese

1. Heat oven to 350°F.

2. In large bowl, toss pasta, butter, Parmesan and eggs. Spread mixture into 9-inch pie plate. Spread cheese over pasta; top with tomato sauce. Bake 20 minutes. Remove from oven; sprinkle with mozzarella cheese. Bake an additional 5 minutes or until cheese melts. Let rest 15 minutes before serving.

4 servings.

TOMATO CHICKPEA STEW

Russell Calaty
Polk City, Florida

¼ cup olive oil
4 to 6 garlic cloves, crushed
1 (14.5-oz.) can stewed tomatoes
1 tablespoon chopped fresh parsley
1 tablespoon chopped fresh basil
1 (15-oz.) can chickpeas
⅛ teaspoon salt
⅛ teaspoon freshly ground pepper
1 cup macaroni

1. In large skillet, heat oil over medium-high heat until hot. Sauté garlic until light brown. Add tomatoes, parsley, basil and juice from chickpeas. Season with salt and pepper; simmer 20 minutes. Add chickpeas to skillet; simmer an additional 15 minutes. Stir in macaroni; simmer an additional 5 minutes. Sprinkle with freshly grated Parmesan or Romano cheese before serving, if desired.

2 to 4 servings.

Green Chile Stew

GREEN CHILE STEW
Nancy Suske
Kailua, Hawaii

1 tablespoon vegetable oil
1 large onion, diced
1 tablespoon minced garlic
2 lb. pork butt, diced ($^1/_2$ inch)
$^1/_8$ teaspoon salt
$^1/_8$ teaspoon freshly ground pepper
1 tablespoon chili powder
3 (16-oz.) cans reduced-sodium
   chicken broth
2 (4-oz.) cans green chiles, drained
1 large sprig rosemary, chopped
1 to 2 bay leaves
$1^1/_2$ teaspoons paprika
2 tomatoes, diced
1 (14.5-oz.) can diced tomatoes
2 large Yukon Gold potatoes, diced
3 carrots, diced
1 (16-oz.) can kidney beans
1 (15-oz.) can garbanzo beans, rinsed,
   drained

1. In large skillet, heat oil over medium-high heat until hot. Sauté onion until tender. Add garlic and pork; cook until golden brown and pork is no longer pink in center. Season with salt, pepper and chili powder. Cook until most of liquid has evaporated. Add broth, chiles, herbs and paprika.

2. Cover and simmer 1 hour. Stir in tomatoes, potatoes, carrots and beans. Simmer an additional 45 minutes or until vegetables are tender.

10 to 12 servings.

KATE'S TOMATO-CORN CHOWDER
Kate Missett
Gillette, Wyoming

3 tablespoons butter
1 medium onion, chopped
1 garlic clove, minced
1 rib celery, thinly sliced
1 carrot, thinly sliced
6 small red potatoes, unpeeled, diced
1 (14.5-oz.) can chunky tomato sauce
1 (14.5-oz.) can cream-style corn
3 cups water
3 teaspoons beef bouillon granules
$^1/_4$ teaspoon freshly ground pepper
$^1/_2$ teaspoon dried basil
1 tablespoon bacon bits
1 cup wild rice
1 cup milk

1. In large pot, melt butter over medium heat. Sauté onion, garlic, celery and carrot, stirring occasionally, about 10 minutes or until tender. Stir in potatoes, tomato sauce, corn, water, bouillon, pepper, basil and bacon bits.

2. Reduce heat; cover and simmer 45 minutes or until potatoes are fork-tender. Add rice; heat thoroughly. Stir in milk; simmer 8 to 10 minutes or until heated through.

6 ($1^2/_3$ cups) servings.

CHICKEN CHILI

Deanna Jones
Parker, Colorado

6 (1-lb.) boneless skinless chicken
   breast halves
1 teaspoon salt
$^1/_2$ teaspoon freshly ground pepper
$^1/_4$ cup vegetable oil
4 large onions, chopped
10 large garlic cloves, minced
4 (12-oz.) cans beer
4 teaspoons dried oregano
$^1/_2$ cup chili powder
$^1/_4$ cup ground cumin
12 chicken bouillon cubes
$^1/_2$ cup water
2 teaspoons whole coriander seeds
2 (15-oz.) cans tomato sauce
2 (16-oz.) cans kidney beans, drained
1 (16-oz.) can pinto beans, drained

1. Heat oven to 350°F.

2. Season chicken with salt and pepper. Place skin side up 3-quart casserole; add $^1/_2$-inch water. Cover chicken with aluminum foil. Bake 20 to 30 minutes or until internal temperature reaches 160°F. Remove chicken from oven; cool to room temperature. Remove skin and bones; tear meat into 1-inch pieces. Set aside.

3. In Dutch oven, heat oil over medium-high heat until hot. Sauté onions and garlic until soft. Add beer, oregano, chili powder, cumin, bouillon cubes, water, coriander and tomato sauce; bring to a boil over medium-high heat. Reduce heat to low and simmer, uncovered, $1^1/_2$ hours, stirring occasionally. Stir in beans; simmer an additional 30 minutes. Stir in chicken. Serve with cheese, olives, tomatoes, onions and sour cream, if desired.

12 servings.

TORTELLINI SOUP

Razan Rawa
Chino Hills, California

3 tablespoons butter
2 garlic cloves, minced
2 medium ribs celery, chopped
1 small onion, chopped
1 medium carrot, chopped
8 cups reduced-sodium chicken broth
4 cups water
2 (10-oz.) pkg. dried cheese-filled
   tortellini
2 tablespoons chopped fresh parsley
$^1/_2$ teaspoon freshly ground pepper
1 teaspoon freshly grated nutmeg

1. In Dutch oven, melt butter over medium heat. Sauté garlic, celery, onion and carrot until onion is tender. Stir in broth and water; heat to a boil. Reduce heat and stir in tortellini. Cover and simmer 20 minutes or until tender, stirring occasionally.

2. Stir in parsley, pepper and nutmeg. Cover and cook 10 minutes. Sprinkle with freshly grated Parmesan cheese, if desired. Serve with Italian bread, if desired.

8 servings.

VENISON CHILI

Jeanette D. Sandstrom
Kettering, Ohio

2 lb. ground venison
2 garlic cloves, minced
1 large white onion, chopped
1 cup celery, chopped
1 green bell pepper, chopped
1 tablespoon plus 1$\frac{1}{2}$ teaspoons
  chopped fresh parsley
1 (28-oz.) can diced tomatoes
1 (28-oz.) can tomato sauce
2 (15-oz.) cans red kidney beans
2 tablespoons chili powder
1 teaspoon ground cumin
$\frac{1}{2}$ teaspoon celery salt
1 teaspoon salt
$\frac{1}{8}$ teaspoon garlic salt
$\frac{1}{8}$ teaspoon freshly ground pepper

1. In large saucepan, fry venison and garlic over medium-high heat until venison is no longer pink in center. Stir in onion, celery and bell pepper; cook until celery is crisp-tender. Add tomatoes, sauce, beans and spices; mix well.

2. Cook 1 hour over low heat, stirring frequently. Cover and refrigerate overnight. To serve, heat thoroughly. Sprinkle with cheddar cheese.

8 servings.

COUNTRY LIMA BEAN AND CABBAGE SOUP

Victoria Miller
Philadelphia, Pennsylvania

1 lb. dried baby lima beans, rinsed
8 cups reduced-sodium chicken broth
1 onion, chopped
1 teaspoon chopped fresh marjoram
1 garlic clove, minced
$\frac{1}{2}$ teaspoon crushed red pepper
$\frac{1}{2}$ teaspoon salt, if desired
$\frac{1}{8}$ teaspoon freshly ground pepper
3 cups shredded green cabbage

1. In slow cooker, combine beans, broth, onion, marjoram, garlic, red pepper, salt, pepper and cabbage. Cover and cook on low heat setting 10 to 11 hours.

8 servings.

MAKE-AHEAD SQUASH SOUP

Peggy Kneale
Maitland, Missouri

3 lb. zucchini, sliced
2 cups water
1 (14.5-oz.) can reduced-sodium beef
  broth
1 cup chopped onion
1$\frac{1}{2}$ teaspoons salt
$\frac{1}{8}$ teaspoon garlic powder
1 cup half-and-half

1. In large pot, combine zucchini, water, broth, onion, salt and garlic powder; bring to a boil over medium-high heat. Reduce heat and simmer 20 minutes or until zucchini is tender. Cool slightly. Transfer mixture to food processor; puree until smooth. Transfer soup base to large saucepan; add half-and-half. Cook over medium heat until heated through. Top with cheese and bacon, if desired.

12 servings.

KATE MISSETT'S SICILIAN PASTA CASSEROLE

Kate Missett
Gillette, Wyoming

1 lb. lean ground beef
2 tablespoons olive oil
4 medium carrots, finely diced
1 large onion, finely diced
$^1/_4$ lb. mushrooms, finely diced
3 cups spaghetti sauce
$^2/_3$ cup red wine
$1^1/_2$ teaspoons salt
$1^1/_2$ teaspoons sugar
$1^1/_2$ teaspoons dried basil
$1^1/_2$ teaspoons dried oregano
$^1/_2$ teaspoon freshly ground pepper
$^1/_2$ teaspoon garlic powder
1 (10-oz.) pkg. frozen chopped
   spinach, thawed
1 (6 oz.) pkg. spinach noodles
$1^1/_2$ cups (6 oz.) grated colby cheese

1. Heat oven to 375°F. Spray 13x9-inch pan with nonstick cooking spray.

2. In large skillet, cook beef over medium heat until no longer pink in center; drain. Stir in oil, carrots, onion and mushrooms; sauté 5 minutes, stirring frequently until onion is tender. Add sauce, wine, salt, sugar, basil, oregano, pepper and garlic powder. Cook over low heat, uncovered, 30 minutes, stirring often.

3. Meanwhile, squeeze spinach dry. Cook noodles in boiling water 9 minutes. Drain noodles; mix thoroughly with spinach.

4. Spread half of the noodle mixture in pan. Top with half of the meat mixture and $^1/_2$ cup of the cheese. Repeat layers; top with remaining 1 cup cheese. Bake, uncovered, 30 minutes or until heated through.

8 to 10 servings.

ITALIAN SAUSAGE AND GREENS SOUP

Colleen Paulson
Hillsboro, Oregon

2 lb. sweet Italian sausage, cut into
   $^1/_2$-inch slices
3 tablespoons olive oil
3 tablespoons unsalted butter
3 large white onions, chopped
6 garlic cloves, thinly sliced
1 teaspoon dried thyme
$^1/_4$ teaspoon crushed red pepper
3 bay leaves
$^3/_4$ cup marsala wine
$1^1/_2$ cups dry white wine
6 cups reduced-sodium chicken broth
2 bunches assorted greens (mustard,
   kale, spinach, etc.)
$^1/_8$ teaspoon salt

1. In large skillet, brown sausages over medium heat. Drain well on paper towels. Set aside.

2. In Dutch oven, heat olive oil and butter over medium-high heat until hot. Sauté onions, garlic, thyme, red pepper and bay leaves 10 minutes or until onions are tender. Stir in marsala and white wines to onion mixture. Bring to a boil and reduce by half. Add broth; return to a boil, then reduce heat to low. Add sausages and greens. Simmer, partially covered, about 45 minutes. Discard bay leaves. Season with salt.

3. Serve in warmed bowls with sourdough bread for dipping, if desired.

8 servings.

Italian Sausage and Greens Soup

CALIFORNIA CASSEROLE

David A. Heppner
Brandon, Florida

2 lb. ground beef
1 medium green bell pepper, chopped
3/4 cup chopped onion
1 (16.5-oz.) can creamed corn
1 (8-oz.) can tomato sauce
1 (10³/4-oz.) can condensed tomato
  soup
1 (4-oz.) can mushrooms
1 (10-oz.) can tomatoes with green
  chiles
1 (2.25-oz.) can sliced ripe olives,
  drained
1 (4-oz.) jar diced pimientos, drained
1¹/2 teaspoons celery salt
1/2 teaspoon chili powder
1/2 teaspoon dry mustard
1/4 teaspoon freshly ground pepper
8 oz. wide egg noodles
2 cups (8 oz.) shredded cheddar
  cheese

1. Heat oven to 350°F. Spray 13x9-inch pan with
nonstick cooking spray.

2. In large skillet, cook beef, bell peppers and onion
until meat is no longer pink in center and onion is
tender; drain. Stir in corn, tomato sauce, soup, mushrooms, tomatoes, olives, pimientos, celery salt, chili
powder, dry mustard and pepper; mix thoroughly.
Add noodles; mix well.

3. Pour mixture into pan. Cover and bake 50 minutes. Sprinkle with cheese. Bake an additional 10
minutes or until cheese melts.

12 to 16 servings.

FALL HARVEST CASSEROLE

Laura Stieglitz
Deep River, Connecticut

2 small zucchini, thinly sliced
4 carrots, thinly sliced
1 medium yellow onion, finely
  chopped
1 large red bell pepper, seeded,
  coarsely chopped
1 lb. ground beef
1 cup white rice
2 cups water
1 (10³/4-oz.) can condensed cream of
  mushroom soup
1 teaspoon low-sodium soy sauce
1/4 teaspoon freshly ground pepper
1 teaspoon dried parsley

1. Heat oven to 375°F. Spray 13x9-inch pan with
nonstick cooking spray.

2. In large bowl, combine zucchini, carrots, onion,
bell pepper, beef, rice, water, mushroom soup, soy
sauce, pepper and parsley; mix well. Stir mixture into
pan. Cover with aluminum foil. Bake 1 hour. Serve
with warm bread and butter, if desired.

6 to 8 servings.

SCALLOPED SALMON

Delia Kennedy
Deer Park, Washington

$^1/_3$ cup all-purpose flour
$^1/_4$ cup butter
3 cups milk
$^1/_8$ teaspoon freshly ground pepper
1 (16-oz.) can boneless salmon, cut
   into 1-inch pieces
4 eggs
1$^1/_2$ cups crushed butter crackers
6 oz. egg noodles

1. Heat oven to 375°F. Spray 13x9-inch pan with nonstick cooking spray.

2. Combine flour, butter and milk in medium bowl; mix well. Season with pepper. In large bowl, combine salmon and eggs; mix slightly. Pour flour mixture into salmon mixture; toss gently.

3. In small bowl, combine crumbs and butter until mixture crumbles.

4. Stir salmon mixture into pan; cover with crumb mixture. Bake 1 hour or until lightly browned and salmon flakes easily with fork. Serve over noodles.

6 to 8 servings.

CHICKEN TACO CASSEROLE

Loretta Abrams
Phoenix, Arizona

4 (1-lb.) bone-in chicken breast
   halves, cooked, bones removed,
   cut into 1-inch pieces
1 (19-oz.) can mild enchilada sauce
1 (10$^3/_4$-oz.) can condensed cream of
   chicken soup
1 (4-oz.) can chopped green chiles
1 small onion, diced
8 cups corn chips
3 cups (12 oz.) shredded cheddar
   cheese
1 cup reduced-sodium chicken broth

1. Heat oven to 400°F. Spray 3-quart casserole with nonstick cooking spray.

2. In large bowl, combine enchilada sauce with soup; mix well. Slowly add $^1/_2$ cup of the broth. Add chiles, onion and chicken; mix thoroughly.

3. Layer bottom of pan with 4 cups of the corn chips. Top with half of the chicken mixture, 1$^1/_2$ cups cheese, remaining 4 cups chips and remaining chicken mixture. Sprinkle with remaining 1$^1/_2$ cups cheese. Top with remaining $^1/_2$ cup broth.

4. Bake 30 minutes or until hot and bubbly. Serve with tossed salad.

6 to 8 servings.

NOTE The top cheese layer can be added last 5 minutes of bake time.

Friday Potato Pie

FRIDAY POTATO PIE

Debbie Patt
Holley, New York

1 (9-inch) unbaked pie shell
6 to 8 medium potatoes, thinly sliced
2 large onions, thinly sliced
3 green bell peppers, thinly sliced
$1/4$ lb. white American cheese, thinly
   sliced
$1/4$ cup butter
1 egg, beaten

1. Heat oven to 350°F. Spray 9-inch pie plate with nonstick cooking spray.

2. Place pie shell in plate. Arrange thin layers of potatoes, onions, bell peppers and cheese in plate; dot with butter. Repeat layers, making sure to heap in center as cooking will shrink down center of pie.

3. Cover edge of pie with 3-inch strip of aluminum foil to prevent excessive browning. Remove foil during last 15 minutes of baking. Bake 1 hour or until lightly browned.

6 to 8 servings.

SWISSED HAM AND NOODLE CASSEROLE

Michelle Pekrun
Panama City, Florida

2 tablespoons butter
$1/2$ cup chopped onion
$1/2$ cup chopped green bell pepper
1 ($10^3/4$-oz.) can condensed cream of
   mushroom soup
1 cup sour cream
8 oz. egg noodles
2 cups (8 oz.) shredded Swiss cheese
2 cups cooked cubed ham

1. Heat oven to 350°F. Spray 2-quart casserole with nonstick cooking spray.

2. In large skillet, melt butter over medium heat; sauté onion and bell pepper until onion is transparent. Remove skillet from heat; stir in soup and sour cream.

3. Meanwhile, layer one-third of the noodles, one-third of the cheese, one-third of the ham and one half the soup mixture in pan. Repeat layers, ending with noodles, ham and cheese. Bake 30 to 45 minutes or until heated through.

6 to 8 servings.

SAUERKRAUT AND SAUSAGE BAKE

Susan M. Bork
Indianapolis, Indiana

1¹/₂ lb. sweet Italian sausage
1 (28-oz.) can sauerkraut, drained
1 tablespoon sliced green onions
¹/₂ cup (2 oz.) freshly grated
   Parmesan cheese
3 cups prepared mashed potatoes

1. Heat oven to 400°F. Spray 3-quart casserole with nonstick cooking spray.

2. In large skillet, heat oil over medium-high heat until hot. Cook sausage until no longer pink in center; drain well. In medium bowl, combine sauerkraut and green onion; toss gently. Place sauerkraut in bottom of casserole; top with sausage.

3. Stir ¹/₄ cup of the cheese into prepared potatoes. Spread potatoes over top of sausage. Sprinkle with remaining ¹/₄ cup cheese. Bake 35 to 40 minutes or until potatoes are just brown. Serve with fruit salad and sauerkraut rye bread, if desired.

6 servings.

MUSHROOM-CHICKEN BAKE

Audrey Derr
Valrico, Florida

4 (1-lb.) boneless skinless chicken
   breast halves
4 (1-oz.) slices Monterey Jack cheese
1 (10³/₄-oz.) can condensed cream of
   mushroom soup
¹/₂ cup cooking sherry or dry white
   wine
2 cups herb-seasoned stuffing mix
¹/₂ cup butter, melted

1. Heat oven to 350°F. Spray 8-inch square pan with nonstick cooking spray.

2. Place chicken in pan; top with cheese. In large saucepan, combine soup and sherry in saucepan; bring to a boil over medium heat. Pour over chicken.

3. In medium bowl, combine stuffing mix and butter; mix well. Spoon stuffing mixture evenly over chicken. Bake, uncovered, 1 hour or until golden brown and internal temperature reaches 160°F..

4 servings.

CHEESE-CHICKEN CASSEROLE

Russell Calaty–Polk City, Florida

1 (1-lb.) boneless skinless chicken
   breast halves, cut into 1-inch pieces
¹/₄ cup chopped onion
2 ribs celery, sliced
1 tablespoon butter
1 (10³/₄-oz.) can condensed cream of
   chicken soup
1 ¹/₃ cups water
¹/₂ lb. diced American cheese
¹/₄ teaspoon freshly ground pepper
1 (8 oz.) pkg. cooked rotini
¹/₂ cup Italian-style bread crumbs
1 tablespoon butter

1. Heat oven to 350°F. Spray 3-quart casserole with nonstick cooking spray.

2. In large skillet, melt butter over medium heat. Sauté onion and celery until onion is transparent; add chicken. Cook mixture until chicken is no longer pink in center. Stir in soup, water and cheese; season with pepper. Cook over low heat until cheese is melted. Stir in pasta. Pour mixture into casserole. Sprinkle with bread crumbs and dot with butter. Bake 30 minutes.

6 servings.

FAMILY-STYLE HOT DOGS WITH RED BEANS AND RICE

Tammy Raynes
Natchitoches, Louisiana

1 tablespoon vegetable oil
1 medium onion, chopped
$1/2$ cup chopped green bell pepper
2 garlic cloves, minced
1 (14-oz.) can red kidney beans, drained
1 (14-oz.) can great Northern beans, drained, rinsed
$1/2$ lb. beef hot dogs, cut into $1/4$-inch thick slices
1 cup instant brown rice
1 cup reduced-sodium vegetable broth
$1/4$ cup ketchup
$1/4$ cup packed brown sugar
3 tablespoons dark molasses
1 tablespoon Dijon mustard

1. Heat oven to 350°F. Spray 13x9-inch pan with nonstick cooking spray.

2. In Dutch oven, heat oil over medium-high heat until hot. Sauté onion, bell pepper and garlic 4 minutes or until onion is tender. Add beans, hot dogs, rice, broth, ketchup, brown sugar, molasses and mustard; stir to combine.

3. Pour mixture into pan. Cover tightly with aluminum foil. Bake 30 minutes or until rice is tender. Garnish with zucchini ribbons.

6 servings.

SAVORY VEGETARIAN LENTIL LOAF

Kathy Hickey
Ashley, Pennsylvania

1 cup lentils
$2^{1}/_4$ cups water
2 tablespoons oil
1 onion, chopped
1 rib celery, chopped
1 cup sliced mushrooms
2 garlic cloves, minced
1 cup dry bread crumbs
1 egg, beaten
$1/2$ teaspoon sage
$1/2$ teaspoon freshly ground pepper
$1/2$ teaspoon thyme
3 hard-cooked eggs, sliced
$1/4$ cup chile sauce

1. Heat oven to 350°F. Spray 9x5-inch loaf pan with nonstick cooking spray.

2. In medium pot, cook lentils in water, covered, 1 hour or until all liquid evaporates.

3. In large skillet, heat oil over medium-high heat until hot. Sauté onion, celery, mushroom and garlic until onion is tender. Transfer mixture to large bowl. Add lentils, bread crumbs, egg, sage, pepper and thyme; toss gently.

4. Place half of lentil mixture into pan. Arrange egg slices down center. Cover with remaining lentil mixture. Spread with chili sauce.

5. Bake 50 minutes. Cool 5 minutes before slicing. Sprinkle with cheese, if desired.

4 to 6 servings.

SHEPHERD'S PIE

Tammy Raynes
Natchitoches, Louisiana

2$^1/_2$ lb. potatoes, peeled, cooked
1 cup sour cream
$^1/_8$ teaspoon salt
$^1/_8$ teaspoon freshly ground pepper
2 lb. ground beef
1 medium red bell pepper, chopped
$^1/_2$ cup chopped onion
1 (15.25-oz.) can whole kernel corn, drained
1 (10$^3/_4$-oz.) can condensed cream of mushroom soup
$^1/_2$ cup milk
1 teaspoon garlic salt
2 tablespoons margarine, melted

1. Heat oven to 350°F. Spray 3-quart casserole with nonstick cooking spray.

2. In large bowl, mash potatoes with sour cream. Season with salt and pepper. Set aside.

3. In large skillet, cook beef, bell pepper and onion until beef is no longer pink in center and onion is tender; drain. Stir in corn, soup, milk and garlic salt; mix well.

4. Spread meat mixture into casserole. Top with mashed potatoes; drizzle with margarine. Bake, uncovered, 30 to 35 minutes or until heated through. For additional browning, place under broiler 2 to 3 minutes. Sprinkle with parsley, if desired.

8 to 10 servings.

MEXICAN ROLL-UPS WITH AVOCADO SAUCE

Tammy Raynes
Natchitoches, Louisiana

1 tablespoon butter
8 eggs
2 tablespoons milk
1$^1/_2$ cups (6 oz.) shredded Monterey Jack cheese
1 large tomato, seeded, chopped
$^1/_4$ cup chopped fresh cilantro
8 (6-inch) corn or flour tortillas
1$^1/_2$ cups salsa
2 medium avocados, chopped
$^1/_4$ cup sour cream
2 tablespoons diced green chiles
1 tablespoon fresh lemon juice
1 teaspoon hot pepper sauce
$^1/_4$ teaspoon salt

1. Heat oven to 350°F. Spray 13x9-inch pan with nonstick cooking spray.

2. In large skillet, melt butter over medium heat. Whisk eggs and milk in medium bowl until blended. Pour egg mixture into skillet. Cook and stir 5 minutes or until eggs are set but still soft. Remove from heat. Stir in cheese, tomato and cilantro.

3. Spoon $^1/_3$ cup of egg mixture evenly down center of each tortilla. Roll up tortilla and place seam side down in pan. Pour salsa evenly over tortillas. Cover tightly with aluminum foil. Bake 20 minutes or until heated through.

4. Meanwhile, process avocado, sour cream, chiles, lemon juice, hot pepper sauce and salt in food processor or blender until smooth. Serve roll-ups with avocado sauce.

8 servings.

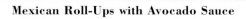
Mexican Roll-Ups with Avocado Sauce

HAM, BARLEY AND ALMOND BAKE

Tammy Raynes
Natchitoches, Louisiana

$^1/_2$ cup slivered almonds
1 tablespoon margarine
1 cup barley
1 cup chopped carrots
1 bunch green onions, sliced
2 ribs celery, sliced
3 garlic cloves, minced
1 lb. lean smoked ham, cubed
2 teaspoons dried basil
1 teaspoon dried oregano
$^1/_4$ teaspoon freshly ground pepper
2 (14-oz.) cans reduced-sodium beef
 broth
$^1/_2$ lb. fresh green beans, cut into
 1-inch pieces

1. Heat oven to 350°F. Spray 13x9-inch pan with nonstick cooking spray.

2. Spread almonds in single layer in pan. Bake 5 minutes or until golden brown, stirring frequently. Set aside.

3. In large skillet, melt margarine over medium-high heat. Sauté barley, carrots, green onion, celery and garlic 4 minutes or until onion is tender. Remove from heat. Stir in ham, almonds, dried basil, oregano and pepper; mix well.

4. In medium saucepan, bring broth to a boil over medium-high heat; pour over barley mixture. Cover pan tightly with aluminum foil. Bake 20 minutes. Remove from oven. Stir in green beans. Bake, covered, an additional 30 minutes or until barley is tender. Garnish with fresh basil and carrot ribbons.

8 servings.

CHILI MEATLOAF AND POTATO CASSEROLE

Tammy Raynes
Natchitoches, Louisiana

MEAT LOAF
$1^1/_2$ lb. lean ground beef
$^3/_4$ cup finely chopped onion
$^1/_3$ cup crushed butter crackers
1 egg, slightly beaten
3 tablespoons milk
1 tablespoon chili powder
$^3/_4$ teaspoon salt

POTATO TOPPING
3 cups prepared mashed potatoes
1 (1-oz.) can whole kernel corn with
 red and green peppers, drained
$^1/_4$ cup thinly sliced green onions
1 cup (4 oz.) shredded taco-seasoned
 cheese

1. Heat oven to 375°F. Spray 8-inch square pan with nonstick cooking spray.

2. In large bowl, combine beef, onion, crumbs, egg, milk, chili powder and salt; mix well. Gently press mixture into bottom of pan. Bake 20 to 25 minutes or until internal temperature reaches 160°F. Carefully pour off juices.

3. Meanwhile, heat broiler. Combine prepared potatoes, corn and green onions in medium bowl; mix well. Spread potato mixture over meat loaf to edges of pan; sprinkle with cheese. Broil 4 to 6 inches from heat 3 to 5 minutes or until top is lightly browned.

6 servings.

LAMB-NOODLE STROGANOFF

Tammy Raynes
Natchitoches, Louisiana

2 lb. ground lamb
2 garlic cloves, minced
1 (15-oz.) can tomato sauce
1 teaspoon salt
$1/4$ teaspoon freshly ground pepper
12 oz. egg noodles
1 (8-oz.) pkg. cream cheese, softened
2 cups sour cream
6 green onions, sliced
$1^1/2$ (6 oz.) cups shredded cheddar cheese
$1/8$ teaspoon paprika

1. Heat oven to 350°F. Spray 13x9-inch pan with nonstick cooking spray.

2. In large skillet, sauté lamb and garlic until meat is no longer pink in center; drain. Stir in tomato sauce, salt and pepper; simmer, uncovered, 10 minutes. Place noodles in pan. Top with meat mixture.

3. In small bowl, beat cream cheese and sour cream at medium speed until smooth; stir in green onions. Spread over meat mixture. Bake, uncovered, 30 minutes or until heated through. Sprinkle with cheese and paprika. Let stand 5 minutes.

8 to 10 servings.

MEXICAN TURKEY ROLL-UPS

Tammy Raynes
Natchitoches, Louisiana

$2^1/2$ cups cooked cubed turkey
$1^1/2$ cups sour cream
1 ($10^3/4$-oz.) can condensed cream of mushroom soup
3 teaspoons taco seasoning, divided
$1^1/2$ cups (6 oz.) shredded cheddar cheese
1 small onion, chopped
$1/2$ cup salsa
$1/4$ cup sliced ripe olives
10 (7-inch) flour tortillas

1. Heat oven to 350°F. Spray 13x9-inch pan with nonstick cooking spray.

2. In medium bowl, combine turkey, $1/2$ cup of the sour cream, one half of the soup, $1^1/2$ teaspoons of the taco seasoning, 1 cup of the cheese, onion, salsa and olives. Spoon $1/3$ cup of mixture on each tortilla. Roll up; place seam side down in pan.

3. Combine remaining 1 cup sour cream, remaining soup and remaining $1^1/2$ teaspoons taco seasoning; pour over tortillas. Cover and bake 30 minutes or until heated through. Sprinkle with remaining $1/2$ cup cheese. Garnish with lettuce, tomatoes and olives. Serve with salsa.

5 servings.

Back Bay Chicken

BACK BAY CHICKEN

Marsha Kay Clow
Crookston, Minnesota

CHICKEN
1 (3- to 4-lb.) broiler-fryer chicken,
  cut up
$1^1/2$ tablespoons butter
$^1/4$ cup chopped green onion
$^1/2$ cup chopped green bell pepper
$^1/2$ carrot, thinly sliced
1 ($10^3/4$-oz.) can condensed cream of
  mushroom soup
$^1/4$ cup dry white wine
1 cup water
1 pimiento, chopped
$^1/3$ cup coarsely chopped roasted red
  bell pepper

BISCUITS
1 cup all-purpose flour
$^1/2$ cup cornmeal
$1^1/2$ teaspoons sugar
2 teaspoons baking powder
$^1/2$ teaspoon salt
3 tablespoons shortening
$^3/4$ cup milk

1. Heat oven to 375°F. Spray Dutch oven with non-stick cooking spray.

2. Rinse chicken and pat dry.

3. In large skillet, melt butter over medium heat; brown chicken. Transfer chicken to Dutch oven. In same skillet, sauté bell pepper, carrot and green onion in pan juices 3 minutes. Add soup, wine and water; heat until mixture bubbles. Add pimiento; pour over chicken and cover. Bake 1 hour.

4. Meanwhile, prepare biscuits. In large bowl, combine flour, cornmeal, sugar, baking powder, salt, shortening and milk; mix well until soft dough forms. Cover dough with clean kitchen towel; set aside.

5. Increase heat to 425°F. Drop biscuit dough by tablespoons around edge of chicken stew. Bake, uncovered, 15 minutes or until dumplings are golden brown.

6 servings

BEEF AND BLACK-EYED PEA CASSEROLE

Tammy Raynes
Natchitoches, Louisiana

1 lb. ground beef
1 large garlic clove, minced
2 (15-oz.) cans black-eyed peas with
  jalapeño chiles, drained
1 (16-oz.) can whole chopped
  tomatoes, drained
2 cups cooked rice
1 cup (4 oz.) shredded sharp cheddar
  cheese
$^1/2$ cup minced onion
1 tablespoon margarine, melted
$^1/2$ teaspoon salt
$^1/2$ teaspoon freshly ground pepper

1. Heat oven to 350°F. Spray 13x9-inch pan with nonstick cooking spray.

2. In large skillet, cook beef and garlic over medium heat, stirring frequently until meat is no longer pink in center. Drain and place in large bowl. Add peas, tomatoes, rice, cheese, onion, margarine, salt and pepper; stir well.

3. Pour mixture into pan. Bake, uncovered, 20 minutes.

8 servings.

SPAGHETTI CASSEROLE

Tammy Raynes
Natchitoches, Louisiana

$^{1}/_{2}$ lb. spaghetti
1 large egg
$^{1}/_{2}$ cup milk
1 lb. ground beef
1 medium onion, chopped
1 medium green bell pepper, seeded,
 chopped
1 jalapeño chile, minced
1 large garlic clove, minced
2 teaspoons chili powder
$^{1}/_{2}$ teaspoon dried oregano
$^{1}/_{2}$ teaspoon ground cumin
$^{1}/_{2}$ teaspoon salt
$^{1}/_{4}$ teaspoon freshly ground pepper
1 (16-oz.) can tomato sauce
1 cup (4 oz.) shredded Monterey Jack
 cheese
1 cup (4 oz.) shredded cheddar
 cheese

1. Heat oven to 425°F. Spray 13x9-inch pan with nonstick cooking spray.

2. Place pasta in pan. In large bowl, beat together egg and milk at medium speed until frothy. Pour egg mixture over pasta; toss gently. Set aside.

3. In large skillet, combine beef, onion, bell pepper, jalapeño and garlic over medium heat; cook, stirring occasionally, until meat is no longer pink in center and onion is tender. Drain off excess fat. Stir in chili powder, oregano, cumin, salt and pepper; cook 3 minutes. Add tomato sauce; cook an additional 2 minutes.

4. Spread meat mixture over pasta. Sprinkle with cheeses. Bake 15 minutes or until cheese is melted. Let stand 5 minutes before serving.

4 servings.

NORMA'S EGGPLANT PARMESAN

Norma Gorman
East Falmouth, Massachusetts

1 egg
$^{1}/_{4}$ cup milk
2 cups sliced large mushrooms
1 large eggplant, peeled, cut into
 $^{1}/_{2}$-inch slices
$^{3}/_{4}$ cup whole wheat bread crumbs
3 cups marinara sauce
2 cups (8 oz.) ricotta cheese
6 (1-oz.) slices mozzarella cheese
$^{1}/_{4}$ cup (1-oz.) freshly grated
 Parmesan cheese
2 lb. broccoli, cooked

1. Heat oven to 400°F. Spray 15x10x1-inch baking pan with nonstick cooking spray.

2. In large bowl, beat egg and milk at medium speed until frothy; set aside. Pour bread crumbs into medium bowl; set aside.

3. In large skillet, stir-fry mushrooms until slightly softened; set aside.

4. Dip eggplant slices into egg mixture, then bread crumbs. Place on baking sheet. Bake 25 to 30 minutes or until eggplant is just tender. After removing eggplant, increase oven temperature to 500°F.

5. Place eggplant in 3-quart casserole. Pour $^{1}/_{2}$ cup marinara over each slice. Place small scoop of ricotta in center of each slice; top with mozzarella slice. Sprinkle lightly with cheese, if desired. Arrange broccoli and mushrooms around eggplant. Bake 15 minutes or until cheese is melted and begins to brown.

6 to 8 servings.

BREAKFAST, LUNCH and
PANTRY SUPPERS

BREAKFAST PIZZA

Tammy Raynes
Natchitoches, Louisiana

1 (10-oz.) can refrigerated biscuit
   dough
$1/2$ lb. thick-sliced bacon
2 tablespoons margarine
2 tablespoons all-purpose flour
$1/4$ teaspoon salt
$1/8$ teaspoon freshly ground pepper
$1^1/2$ cups milk
$1/2$ cup (2 oz.) shredded sharp
   cheddar cheese
$1/4$ cup sliced green onions
$1/4$ cup chopped red bell pepper

1. Heat oven to 350°F. Spray 13x9-inch pan with nonstick cooking spray.

2. Separate biscuit dough; arrange side-by-side in rectangle on lightly floured surface without overlapping. Roll into 14x10-inch rectangles. Place in pan; pat edges up sides of dish. Bake 15 minutes; remove and set aside.

3. Meanwhile, in large skillet, cook bacon over medium heat until crisp. Remove from skillet; drain on paper towels. Crumble and set aside.

4. In medium saucepan, melt margarine over medium heat. Stir in flour, salt and pepper; mix until smooth. Gradually stir in milk and cheese; heat until thickened and cheese is melted. Spread evenly over baked crust. Sprinkle with bacon, green onions and bell pepper.

5. Bake, uncovered, 20 minutes or until crust is golden brown.

6 servings.

RICE AND CHICKPEAS

Bonnie L. Austin
Kinder, Louisiana

4 cups boiling water
2 cups rice
1 teaspoon ground cumin
1 teaspoon ground allspice
$1/2$ teaspoon ground cinnamon
1 (15-oz.) can cooked chickpeas,
   drained
1 teaspoon salt

1. In large pot, bring water to a boil. Add rice, cumin, allspice, cinnamon, chickpeas and salt. Reduce heat to low; cover and simmer 20 minutes or until all liquid is absorbed. Turn off heat; let stand, covered, 5 minutes.

2. Fluff rice mixture with fork. Garnish with parsley. Serve with yogurt and cucumber salad, if desired.

6 servings.

Rice and Chickpeas

McCAJUN CASSEROLE

Tom Dellostritto
Auburn, New York

$^1/_2$ lb. thick-sliced bacon
6 eggs
$^1/_8$ teaspoon salt
$^1/_8$ teaspoon freshly ground pepper
$1^1/_2$ cups buttermilk baking mix
1 cup milk
2 cups (8 oz.) grated sharp cheddar
 cheese
$^1/_2$ cup chopped onion
1 teaspoon Cajun spice seasoning

1. Heat oven to 350°F. Spray 2-quart casserole with nonstick cooking spray.

2. In large skillet, cook bacon over medium-high heat until crisp; remove from heat. Crumble bacon; set aside. In medium bowl, beat eggs at medium speed until frothy; season with salt and pepper. Stir in bacon, baking mix, milk, cheese, onion and Cajun seasoning; mix well.

3. Pour mixture into casserole. Bake 45 minutes or until eggs are set.

4 to 6 servings.

NOTE You can add nearly anything to this recipe. Try bell peppers, cooked mushrooms, cooked Italian sausage, 1 teaspoon dry mustard and/or a few drops of hot pepper sauce.

SAUSAGE & EGG CASSEROLE

Tammy Raynes
Natchitoches, Louisiana

1 lb. pork sausage
6 eggs
2 cups milk
1 teaspoon salt
1 teaspoon dry mustard
6 slices white bread, cut into $^1/_2$-inch
 pieces
1 cup (4 oz) grated cheddar cheese

1. Heat oven to 350°F. Spray 11x7-inch baking dish with nonstick cooking spray.

2. In large skillet, cook sausage until brown; crumble and drain. In large bowl, beat eggs; add milk, salt and mustard. Stir in bread, cheese and sausage; mix well.

3. Pour mixture into baking dish. Cover and refrigerate at least 8 hours or overnight. Remove from refrigerator 30 minutes before baking. Bake, uncovered, 40 to 50 minutes or until knife inserted near center comes out clean.

8 to 10 servings.

SEAFOOD SALAD SANDWICH

Judy Wong-Burk–Oakland, California

1 (7-oz.) pkg. cooked shrimp
1 (7-oz.) pkg. cooked shredded
 crabmeat
2 ribs celery, finely chopped
$^1/_2$ cup chopped ripe olives
$^1/_2$ cup mayonnaise
4 teaspoons butter, softened
8 slices bread
4 (1-oz.) slices cheese

1. In small bowl, combine shrimp, crabmeat, celery, olives and mayonnaise; mix well. Butter 4 slices of bread; spread 1 cup seafood mixture on each slice of bread. Top each with 1 slice cheese. Cut sandwich in half and serve with fruit, if desired.

4 servings.

BREAKFAST BURRITOS

Tammy Raynes
Natchitoches, Louisiana

1 (16-oz.) pkg. frozen Southern-style
    hash brown potatoes
12 eggs
1 onion, chopped
1 green bell pepper, chopped
1/2 lb. bulk sausage, cooked, drained
12 (10-inch) flour tortillas
3 cups (12 oz.) shredded cheddar
    cheese

1. Heat oven to 350°F. Spray 15x10x1-inch baking pan with nonstick cooking spray.

2. In large nonstick skillet, fry hash browns according to package directions; remove and set aside.

3. In large bowl, beat eggs at medium speed until frothy; add onion and bell pepper. Pour into same skillet; cook, stirring occasionally, until eggs are set. Remove from heat. Add hash browns and sausage to skillet; cook 5 to 7 minutes or until sausage is heated through.

4. Place about 3/4 cup mixture on tortilla; top with 1/4 cup cheese. Roll up and place on baking sheet. Bake, uncovered, 15 to 20 minutes or until heated through. Serve with salsa, if desired.

12 servings.

BREAKFAST CASSEROLE

Rebecca Ciero
Des Plaines, Illinois

6 English muffins, halved
12 slices Canadian bacon
12 eggs
1/8 teaspoon salt
1/8 teaspoon freshly ground pepper
2 (10³/4-oz.) cans condensed cream of
    mushroom soup
1 cup (4 oz) shredded cheddar cheese

1. Heat oven to 350°F. Spray 11x14-inch pan with nonstick cooking spray.

2. Line bottom of pan with split muffins. Place 1 slice bacon on each muffin.

3. In medium bowl, beat eggs, salt and pepper at medium speed until frothy. Pour egg mixture evenly over bacon. Spread soup over bacon; sprinkle with cheese. Cover and refrigerate overnight. Bake, covered, 1 hour or until eggs are set.

6 to 12 servings.

PAN PANCAKES

Leane Sears—Elgin, South Carolina

1¹/2 cups buttermilk baking mix
1 tablespoon sugar
2 eggs
3/4 cup milk
1/4 cup maple syrup
1¹/2 cups (6 oz.) shredded cheddar
    cheese
12 thick slices bacon, cooked,
    crumbled

1. Heat oven to 425°F. Spray 13x9-inch pan with nonstick cooking spray.

2. In large bowl, beat baking mix, sugar, eggs, milk, syrup and 1/2 cup of the cheese at medium speed until thoroughly mixed. Pour mixture into pan. Bake, uncovered, 10 to 15 minutes or until set. Sprinkle with remaining 1 cup cheese and bacon. Bake an additional 3 to 5 minutes or until cheese is melted.

6 to 8 servings.

Pumpkin-Pecan Pancakes

PUMPKIN-PECAN PANCAKES

Catherine Livezey
Auburn, California

13 tablespoons vegetable oil
2 cups all-purpose flour
2 tablespoons packed brown sugar
1 tablespoon baking powder
1 teaspoon each salt, cinnamon
$1/4$ teaspoon nutmeg
$1/4$ teaspoon ground ginger
$1^1/2$ cups milk
$1/2$ cup cooked mashed pumpkin
   (not pumpkin pie mix)
1 egg, slightly beaten
$1/2$ cup chopped pecans

1. Heat griddle to 375°F. Pour 1 tablespoon of the oil over griddle.

2. In large bowl, combine flour, brown sugar, baking powder, salt, cinnamon, nutmeg and ginger; mix well. In separate bowl, combine milk, pumpkin, egg and remaining 2 tablespoons oil; mix well. Add flour mixture, stirring until just moistened. Stir in nuts.

3. For each pancake, pour $1/4$ cup batter onto griddle. Using spatula, spread batter into 4-inch circle before mixture sets. Cook until bubbles form on surface and pancake appears dry. Turn and cook an additional 2 to 3 minutes or until pancake is browned. Serve hot with pecan-maple syrup.

16 pancakes.

GRILLED HAM AND EGG SALAD SANDWICHES

Tammy Raynes
Natchitoches, Louisiana

6 hard-cooked eggs, chopped
1 cup diced cooked ham
$1/2$ cup diced celery
$1/2$ cup mayonnaise
1 tablespoon diced onion
2 teaspoons mustard
$1/2$ teaspoon salt
$1/4$ teaspoon freshly ground pepper
12 slices bread
$1/2$ cup cornmeal
$1/2$ cup all-purpose flour
2 cups milk
2 eggs, beaten
2 tablespoons vegetable oil

1. In large bowl, combine hard-cooked eggs, ham, celery, mayonnaise, onion, mustard, salt and pepper; mix well. Spread mixture over 6 slices of the bread. Top with remaining 6 slices bread. In another large bowl, whisk cornmeal, flour, milk and eggs until well blended. In large skillet, heat oil over medium-high heat until hot. Dip sandwiches into batter. Fry 3 minutes per side or until golden brown. Drain on paper towels before serving.

6 sandwiches.

CHICKEN ROLL-UPS

Sandy Zimmerman–Jamestown, Kentucky

1 (8-oz.) can refrigerated crescent
   dinner rolls
4 (1-lb.) boneless skinless chicken
   breast halves, cooked, cut into
   1-inch pieces
4 slices cooked ham ($1/8$ inch thick)
4 (1-oz.) slices Swiss cheese

1. Heat oven to 350°F. Spray baking sheet with non-stick cooking spray. Unroll and press dough into 4 equal squares. Place 1 piece each chicken, ham and cheese on each square; roll up. Pinch ends together to seal. Place on baking sheet. Bake 15 minutes or until golden brown.

4 servings.

STEAK & ONION STUFFERS

Janice Goodner
Macomb, Oklahoma

$^{1}/_{3}$ cup olive oil
2 garlic cloves, minced
3 tablespoons low-sodium soy sauce
$^{1}/_{4}$ teaspoon freshly ground pepper
$^{1}/_{4}$ teaspoon salt
1 teaspoon sesame oil
1 ($1^{1}/_{2}$ lb.) beef tenderloin, thinly sliced
1 large onion, halved lengthwise, thinly sliced
3 pita breads, halved

1. In large resealable plastic bag, combine olive oil, garlic, soy sauce, pepper, salt, sesame oil and beef; seal bag. Place bag in refrigerator; marinate 2 hours.

2. Remove tenderloin from marinade. Heat oven to 350°F. Transfer 3 tablespoons of the marinade into large skillet; sauté onions over medium-high heat 10 minutes or until tender. Remove onions; set aside. Add tenderloin to skillet; sauté 2 minutes or until meat is no longer pink in center. Stir in onions. Heat bread in oven 10 minutes before filling sandwiches.

6 servings.

RANCHERO BEEF PIZZA

David A. Heppner
Brandon, Florida

1 (12-inch) Italian bread shell
3 cups (12 oz.) shredded smoked cheddar cheese
1 lb. cooked shredded barbecued beef
4 slices red onion, separated into rings

1. Heat oven to 400°F. Place bread on ungreased 12-inch pizza pan. Sprinkle with 1 cup of the cheese, beef and onion; top with remaining 2 cups cheese. Bake 15 to 20 minutes or until hot and cheese is melted.

6 servings.

HAM AND ASPARAGUS PIZZA

David A. Heppner
Brandon, Florida

1 (12-inch) Italian bread shell
$^{1}/_{4}$ cup olive oil
$^{1}/_{4}$ teaspoon garlic powder
1 (8-oz.) container plain yogurt
$^{1}/_{2}$ cup (2 oz.) freshly grated Parmesan cheese
1 (15-oz.) can asparagus spears, drained
2 slices smoked ham ($^{1}/_{4}$ inch thick)
$^{1}/_{2}$ cup chopped onion
1 cup (4 oz.) shredded part-skim mozzarella cheese

1. Heat oven to 425°F.

2. Brush bread lightly with oil; sprinkle with garlic powder. Bake 8 minutes; remove from oven and set aside. In medium bowl, combine yogurt and Parmesan cheese; mix well. Set aside. Cut 16 asparagus spears into 4-inch pieces; set aside. Chop remaining asparagus; add to yogurt mixture.

3. From center of each slice of ham, cut 8 julienne strips and trim to 4 inches long; set aside. Chop remaining ham; add to yogurt mixture. Add onions to yogurt; stir well to combine.

4. Spread yogurt mixture evenly across pizza crust. Arrange reserved asparagus around crust; place reserved ham between spears. Sprinkle evenly with mozzarella cheese. Bake 15 minutes or until hot and cheese is melted.

6 to 8 servings.

HAYSTACKS

Marsha Kay Clow
Crookston, Minnesota

1 lb. ground beef
2 small onions, chopped
$^1/_2$ teaspoon salt
$^1/_2$ teaspoon freshly ground pepper
2 tablespoons vegetable oil
4 potatoes, shredded
4 hamburger buns, toasted

1. Heat grill.

2. In large bowl, combine beef, one-half of the onions, salt and pepper; mix well. Shape mixture into 4 (1-inch-thick) patties.

3. Place patties on gas grill over medium heat or on charcoal grill 4 to 6 inches from medium coals. Grill patties, covered, about 4 minutes per side or until patties are no longer pink in center.

4. In large skillet, brown potatoes and remaining onions over medium heat 8 to 10 minutes or until potatoes are crispy and onions are tender. Remove from skillet; drain on paper towels. Place patty on bun; top with hash brown-onion mixture and bun.

4 servings.

KATE MISSETT'S FLOATING-THE-RIVER FETTUCCINE

Kate Missett
Gillette, Wyoming

1 ($10^3/_4$-oz.) can condensed broccoli
   and cheddar soup
$^1/_2$ cup milk
1 (8-oz.) container sour cream
1 teaspoon dried onion
$^1/_2$ teaspoon chopped garlic
$^1/_8$ teaspoon freshly ground pepper
$^1/_4$ cup (1 oz.) freshly grated
   Parmesan cheese
1 lb. cooked chicken, cubed
2 plum tomatoes, sliced, halved
4 large mushrooms, sliced
1 cup fresh broccoli florets
$^1/_4$ cup slivered almonds if desired
8 oz. spinach fettuccine

1. In large skillet, combine soup, milk, sour cream, onion and garlic; heat and stir over medium heat until sour cream is melted. Add pepper, cheese, chicken, tomatoes, mushrooms, broccoli and almonds; bring to a hard simmer. Reduce heat; simmer 5 minutes. Add fettuccine; heat through.

4 servings.

SUPER MAC & CHEESE

Jennifer Gumm–Killeen, Texas

1 cup water
1 (14.5-oz.) can reduced-sodium
   chicken broth
1 (7-oz.) pkg. elbow macaroni
1 (10-oz.) pkg. frozen broccoli florets
$^3/_4$ cup (3 oz.) grated cheddar cheese
3 tablespoons freshly grated Parmesan
   cheese

1. In medium saucepan, bring water and broth to a rolling boil. Remove from heat; add macaroni. Return saucepan to heat. Cook 8 to 10 minutes or until macaroni is tender and slight amount of broth remains. Do not drain. Meanwhile, prepare broccoli according to package directions. Add broccoli and cheese to cooked macaroni; toss gently. Sprinkle with Parmesan cheese just before serving.

4 ($1^1/_2$-cup) servings.

MUCHO VEGGIE PIZZA

Diane Kuhlman
Maryville, Tennessee

2 (8-oz.) cans refrigerated crescent
   dinner rolls
2 (8-oz.) pkg. cream cheese, softened
1 (0.4 oz.) pkg. dry ranch dressing
   mix
1¼ cups shredded vegetables
   (cauliflower, carrots, summer
   squash, celery, etc.)
1 cup chopped fresh tomatoes
1 (4-oz.) can diced green chiles,
   drained
1 tablespoon chili powder
1 cup (4 oz.) shredded cheddar
   cheese
1 cup (4 oz.) shredded Monterey Jack
   cheese

1. Heat oven to 375°F.

2. Place crescent rolls on large nonstick cookie sheet. Press together to remove seams. (Dough should resemble pizza crust.) Cook 8 minutes or until browned. Remove from oven and cool.

3. In large bowl, combine cream cheese and dry ranch mix; stir well. Spread mixture over cooled crust. Sprinkle vegetables over cream cheese; press into cheese. In another large bowl, combine tomatoes, chiles and chili powder; toss gently. Sprinkle mixture over vegetables. Cover with shredded cheeses. Refrigerate 4 to 6 hours before serving. Cut into squares.

8 servings.

ITALIAN DELI SANDWICHES

Tammy Raynes
Natchitoches, Louisiana

2 tablespoons margarine, softened
3 (10-inch) flour tortillas
6 (1-oz.) slices provolone cheese
6 thin slices deli ham
6 thin slices bologna
30 thin slices pepperoni
18 banana pepper rings
9 thin slices tomato
6 lettuce leaves
2 tablespoons mayonnaise

1. Spread margarine on one side of tortillas.

2. Layer each tortilla with cheese, ham, bologna, pepperoni, peppers, tomato and lettuce to within 2 inches of edge; spread mayonnaise over lettuce. Roll up tortilla tightly. Serve immediately or wrap in plastic wrap and refrigerate up to 2 hours.

3 servings.

CHICKEN SALAD FOR SANDWICHES

Tammy Raynes
Natchitoches, Louisiana

2 cups cooked diced chicken
2 hard-cooked eggs, chopped
1 cucumber, diced
1 rib celery, diced
⅓ cup mayonnaise
¼ teaspoon salt
⅛ teaspoon dry mustard
⅛ teaspoon ground white pepper
6 slices bread

1. In large bowl, combine chicken, eggs, cucumber, celery, mayonnaise, salt, dry mustard and pepper; mix well. Serve mixture on bread.

4 to 6 servings.

Chicken Salad for Sandwiches

BAKED SLOPPY JOES

Kelly King
Bismarck, North Dakota

1 lb. ground beef
1 (15.5-oz.) can sloppy joe sauce
$1/4$ cup packed brown sugar
2 tablespoons ketchup
2 cups (8 oz.) shredded cheddar
   cheese
2 cups buttermilk baking mix
2 eggs, beaten
1 cup milk
1 tablespoon sesame seeds

1. Heat oven to 400°F. Spray 13x9-inch pan with nonstick cooking spray.

2. In large skillet, cook beef over medium-high heat until no longer pink in center; drain.

3. Stir in sloppy joe sauce, brown sugar and ketchup; mix well. Pour mixture into pan. Sprinkle cheese over top. In large bowl, combine baking mix, eggs and milk; mix until just blended. Pour over cheese; sprinkle with sesame seeds. Bake, uncovered, about 25 minutes or until cheese is melted.

8 servings.

ISLAND-GRILLED CHICKEN SANDWICH

Elaine Milsaps
Tampa, Florida

MARINADE
$3/4$ cup vegetable oil
$1/2$ cup fresh pineapple juice
$1/8$ teaspoon salt
$1/2$ teaspoon ground cumin
1 tablespoon chopped fresh cilantro
6 slices canned pineapple

SANDWICH
6 (about 1 lb.) boneless skinless
   chicken breast halves
3 to 4 tablespoons olive oil
$3/4$ cup honey mustard
6 hoagie rolls, toasted
$3/4$ cup sliced marinated mushrooms
12 (1-oz.) slices Monterey Jack cheese

1. In large resealable plastic bag, combine oil, juice, salt, cumin and cilantro; blend well with fork. Add pineapple slices. Place chicken in marinade; seal bag. Refrigerate 2 hours. Remove chicken from marinade; reserve pineapple slices.

3. In large skillet, heat oil over medium-high heat until hot. Add chicken; cook about 4 minutes per side or until chicken is no longer pink in center. Remove chicken from pan; set aside. Discard remaining oil.

4. In same pan, sauté pineapple slices until golden brown. To assemble sandwich, spread honey mustard on both halves of roll. Place chicken on bottom half; top with pineapple, mushrooms, cheese and top of roll.

6 servings.

CHICKEN BREAST SANDWICH WITH SWEET AND SOUR PEANUT SPREAD

Gini Stoddard
Kapaa, Hawaii

$1/4$ cup peanut butter
2 teaspoons low-sodium soy sauce
$1^1/2$ tablespoons fresh lemon juice
1 tablespoon packed brown sugar
$1/2$ teaspoon cayenne pepper
4 large hamburger buns, lightly toasted*
2 tablespoons butter, softened
$1/2$ lb. cooked boneless skinless chicken breast, sliced diagonally

1. In small bowl, combine peanut butter, soy sauce, lemon juice, brown sugar and cayenne; mix until smooth and well combined.

2. Lightly spread each toasted bun with butter. Generously spread bottom of bun with peanut mixture. Place chicken slices over peanut spread; top with lettuce. Garnish with parsley, radish rose, sweet pickle slice and taco chips.

4 servings.

TIP *Do not use onion buns.

DILLED CHICKEN SALAD

Jim L. Bell
Belmont, California

$3/4$ cup salad dressing or mayonnaise
$1/4$ cup Dijon mustard
1 teaspoon dried dill weed
$1/4$ teaspoon freshly ground pepper
$2^1/2$ cups cooked cubed chicken
3 green onions, sliced
4 large lettuce leaves

1. In medium bowl combine salad dressing, mustard, dill weed and pepper; mix well. Stir in chicken and onions; toss gently. Serve mixture on lettuce leaves or toast.

4 servings.

HOT CHICKEN-FILLED BUNS

Kathy Hickey
Ashley, Pennsylvania

1 cup cooked diced chicken
2 thick slices bacon, cut into 1-inch pieces
$1/2$ cup chopped onions
1 (8-oz.) pkg. sliced mushrooms
2 teaspoons all-purpose flour
1 tablespoon butter
$1/4$ teaspoon salt
$1/4$ teaspoon freshly ground pepper
4 hard rolls

1. Heat oven to 350°F. Spray 15x10x1-inch pan with nonstick cooking spray. In large skillet, cook bacon over medium-high heat until crisp. Add onion to skillet; sauté 2 minutes or until tender. Drain fat. Add mushrooms to skillet; sprinkle with flour and push to side. Add butter to skillet; sauté until mushrooms are browned. Stir in chicken; season with salt and pepper. Cut off tops of rolls; remove soft centers. Divide chicken mixture among rolls. Place on baking sheet with tops tilted on side of rolls. Bake 10 minutes.

4 servings.

Easy Chicken Quesadillas with Peach Salsa

EASY CHICKEN QUESADILLAS WITH PEACH SALSA

Debbie Patt
Holley, New York

SALSA
3 soft peaches, peeled, diced
2 firm peaches, peeled, diced
$1/3$ cup finely chopped red onion
$1/4$ teaspoon salt
3 tablespoons sugar
2 tablespoons rum or fresh orange
   juice

QUESADILLAS
1 tablespoon olive oil
2 boneless skinless chicken breasts,
   cut into $1/4$-inch strips
2 jalapeño chiles
$1/8$ teaspoon freshly ground pepper
$1/8$ teaspoon Creole seasoning
8 (10-inch) flour tortillas
$1/2$ cup (2 oz.) shredded cheddar or
   colby cheese
$1/2$ cup (2-oz.) shredded Monterey
   Jack cheese
$1/4$ cup fresh chives

1. Heat oven to 350°F. Spray 15x10x1-inch pan with nonstick cooking spray.

2. In large bowl, combine peaches and onions; season with salt and sugar. Fold in rum. Refrigerate 1 hour.

3. Heat medium skillet over high heat until hot. Cook chicken, chiles, pepper and creole 12 to 15 minutes or until chicken juices run clear. Remove from heat.

4. Lay 4 tortillas on pan; sprinkle with cheese. Add chicken strips and chives. Cover with remaining 4 tortillas and bake about 4 minutes or until tortillas are warm and cheese is melted. Remove from oven. Cut tortillas into quarters. Mound peach salsa in center of plate. Place quartered tortillas quartered overlapping salsa.

4 servings.

PLEASING POTATOES AND PEAS

Loretta Abrams
Phoenix, Arizona

1 (14.5-oz.) can reduced-sodium
   chicken broth
$1^1/2$ lb. small new potatoes, quartered
2 cups frozen peas
1 (0.87-oz.) pkg. chicken or turkey
   gravy mix
$1/2$ cup water
$1/2$ teaspoon garlic salt
$1/4$ teaspoon ground thyme
$1/2$ cup sour cream
1 lb. cooked cubed ham, chicken or
   turkey

1. In large pot, bring broth to a boil over medium-high heat. Add potatoes; reduce heat and simmer 20 minutes or until fork-tender. Add peas; cook 2 minutes.

2. In small bowl, combine gravy mix and water; blend well. Stir into potatoes mixture. Add garlic salt and thyme. Stir in sour cream and ham; heat through.

6 servings.

BAKED SOUTHWEST SANDWICHES

David A. Heppner
Brandon, Florida

1 (4.25-oz.) can chopped ripe olives, drained
¹/₂ teaspoon chili powder
¹/₂ teaspoon ground cumin
¹/₄ teaspoon salt
¹/₂ cup mayonnaise
¹/₃ cups sour cream
¹/₃ cup chopped green onions
8 slices Italian bread
1 lb. thinly sliced cooked turkey
2 medium tomatoes, thinly sliced
2 ripe avocados, sliced
³/₄ cup (3 oz.) shredded cheddar cheese
³/₄ cup (3 oz.) shredded Monterey Jack cheese

1. Heat oven to 350°F.

2. In large bowl, combine olives, chili powder, cumin and salt; mix well. Set aside 2 tablespoons of the mixture. To remaining mixture add mayonnaise, sour cream and green onions; mix well.

4. Place bread on 15x10x1-inch pan. Spread 1 tablespoon of mayonnaise mixture on each slice. Top with turkey and tomatoes. Spread with another tablespoon of mayonnaise mixture; top with avocados and cheeses. Sprinkle with reserved olive mixture. Bake 15 minutes or until heated through and cheese is melted.

8 servings.

PORK CHOPS HAWAIIAN

Vivian Nikanow
Chicago, Illinois

1 cup vinegar
¹/₂ cup low-sodium soy sauce
1 cup packed brown sugar
2 tablespoons dry mustard
6 garlic cloves, minced
6 pork chops (1 inch thick)

1. In large resealable plastic bag, combine vinegar, soy sauce, brown sugar, mustard and garlic. Place pork chops in marinade; seal bag. Refrigerate 24 hours.

2. Heat oven to 375°. Spray 2-quart casserole with nonstick cooking spray.

3. Remove pork from marinade; discard marinade. Bake pork chops 45 minutes or until slightly pink in center.

6 servings.

QUICK HASH FOR TWO

Tammy Raynes
Natchitoches, Louisiana

2 tablespoons margarine
1 cup cooked diced beef
1 cup cooked diced potato
1 large onion, diced
1 tablespoon minced fresh parsley
¹/₂ cup milk
¹/₈ teaspoon salt
¹/₈ teaspoon freshly ground pepper

1. In large skillet, melt margarine over medium-high heat.

2. In large bowl, combine beef, potato, onion, parsley, milk, salt and pepper; mix well. Add mixture to skillet; toss well. Flatten mixture with metal spatula. Cover and cook until crisp on bottom. Turn and cook other side until brown.

2 servings.

Pork Chops Hawaiian

STUART'S SPAGHETTI WITH SALMON SAUCE

Laura Ladd
Aurora, Oregon

1 (12-oz.) pkg. spaghetti
2 (10³/₄-oz.) cans condensed cream of
   mushroom soup
1¹/₂ (10³/₄-oz.) cans evaporated milk
1 (15.5-oz.) can boneless pink salmon
¹/₂ teaspoon garlic powder
¹/₄ cup (1 oz.) freshly grated
   Parmesan cheese

1. Cook spaghetti according to package directions. Rinse and drain thoroughly. Set aside.

2. In medium saucepan, combine soup and milk; stir and heat until creamy. Add salmon and garlic powder to saucepan; blend well. Heat to just a simmer, stirring occasionally.

3. Divide spaghetti among 6 individual plates. Spoon salmon sauce over spaghetti; top with Parmesan cheese. Serve with side salad, if desired.

6 servings.

CRANBERRY CHICKEN

Melissa Jacobs
Abilene, Texas

4 boneless skinless chicken breast
   halves
1 (8-oz.) bottle Catalina salad dressing
1 (16-oz.) can whole-berry cranberry
   sauce
1 (1-oz.) pkg. onion soup mix

1. Heat oven to 350°F.

2. In large bowl, combine dressing, berries and soup mix; mix well. Place chicken in 13x9-inch pan. Pour mixture over chicken. Bake, covered, 40 minutes or until chicken juices run clear.

4 servings.

CURLY NOODLE PORK SUPPER

Tammy Raynes
Natchitoches, Louisiana

1 tablespoon vegetable oil
1 lb. pork tenderloin, cut into ¹/₄-inch
   strips
1 red bell pepper, cut into 1-inch
   pieces
1 cup chopped fresh broccoli florets
4 green onions, cut into 1-inch pieces
1¹/₂ cups water
2 (3-oz.) pkg. pork Ramen noodle
   soup mix
1 tablespoon minced fresh parsley
1 tablespoon low-sodium soy sauce

1. In large skillet, heat oil over medium-high heat until hot. Cook pork, bell pepper, broccoli and onions until meat is no longer pink in center.

2. Add water, noodles, seasoning packet, parsley and soy sauce to skillet; bring to a boil. Reduce heat; cook 3 to 4 minutes or until noodles are tender.

4 servings.

RECIPE INDEX

GENERAL INDEX

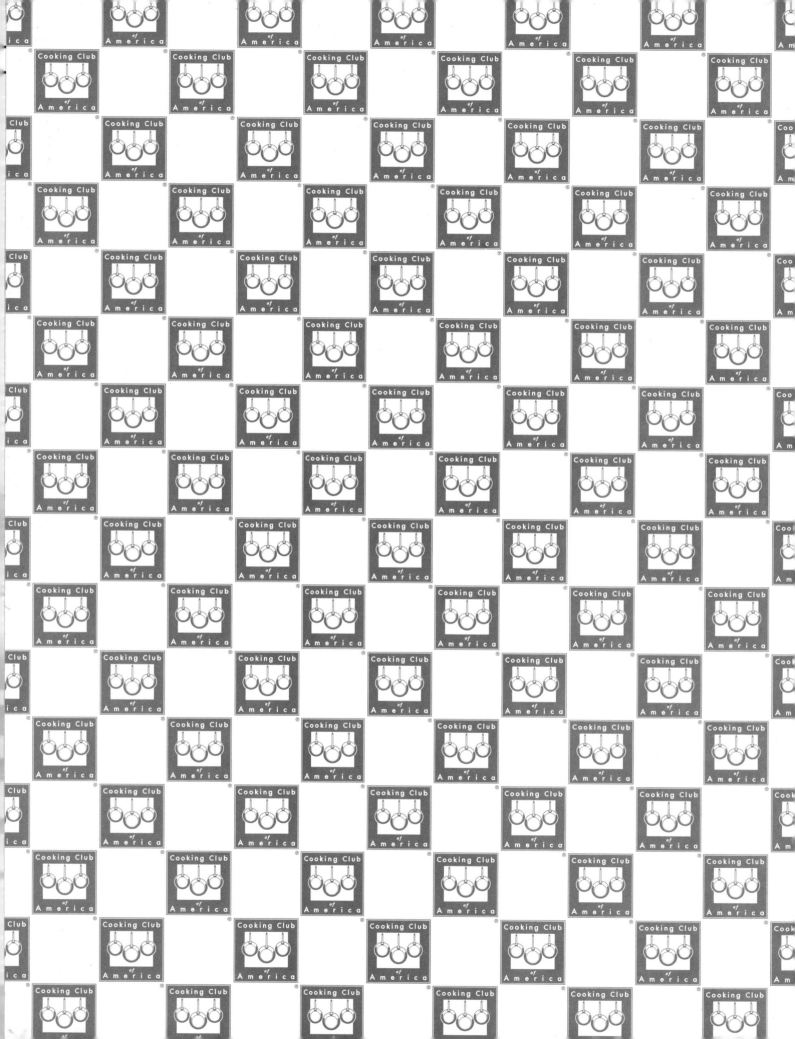